A STORY

IN THE HANDS OF GOD

Encountering Suicide and Miracles

EVAN LIS

Contents

PART 1 YOUR STORY

CHAPTER 1: WHAT IS A STORY?   1

CHAPTER 2: WHAT IS GOD'S STORY?   7

CHAPTER 3: WHAT IS THE REAL STORY?   21

PART 2 MY TESTIMONY

CHAPTER 4: WHAT'S YOUR HEART BEHIND WHAT YOU DO?   29

CHAPTER 5: IN THE BEGINNING   33

CHAPTER 6: DAY-TO-DAY SURVIVAL   37

CHAPTER 7: THE HEART OF SUMMER   43

CHAPTER 8: LET'S BE REAL   53

CHAPTER 9: THE UNQUALIFIED CALLING   57

CHAPTER 10: WHAT'S THE POINT? IS IT EVEN WORTH IT?   65

CHAPTER 11: HOW DO I SHARE MY STORY?   73

CHAPTER 12: THE ATTRACTIVE MIRACLE   83

CONCLUSION   87

AUTHOR'S PRAYER   89

PART 1
Your Story

Chapter 1

What Is a Story?

The first thing that comes to my mind when I think of a story is an experience someone shares that impacts your heart to make you feel a certain way. In other words, the purpose of a story is to give us a sense of connection with the one presenting the story. Whether it's a story in a book, a movie, or a personal account that someone shares, the connecting effect of a story will always impact our hearts in some way. Since stories connect us, let's get right into the big picture. What is the story of my life and your life? Are we simply living through the motions of each day, or is the life we're living set up like a story you would find in a novel or movie? How are we connected with others and with God? Unfortunately, God is not someone that many people want to talk about. Honestly, I think He's someone that people are afraid to talk about. If we don't know Him, we have this natural internal fear when someone mentions Him in conversation and that makes us want to run the other way. That's one thing that sin does to us when it has power over our lives. We need to look at our own life and understand who God is and how we're connected to Him. When we do so, we will likely see that we don't need to run away from Him.

What Is My Story?

To answer this question, you must reflect on what has happened in your life and the events and people affecting your life. How is God using those things in your life? How do we respond to past experiences, and how do those experiences relate to the Word of God? Sometimes, when we intentionally spend time thinking on these things, God can grow us or reveal Himself to us in a new light—almost as if it's the first time we're opening our eyes.

Whether we call it a testimony or a story, every one of us has one. Have you ever asked yourself what's in your story? Of course, there is a beginning and end to your story. In one sense, our story naturally begins when we are born, and it will end the day we die. But in the same way that some books have introductions, it's also true that some stories begin before birth. From beginning to end, every detail in your story is important. We never know when the last page of our story will be written or what it will contain, but we do know how our story began and what has been written so far. It would be nice to assume what the ending will be like based on what has happened, but that's usually not the case.

Different stories are shared for different reasons; it all depends on the author's heart behind the story. But every story has an author, a main character, side characters, a journey, and a purpose that ties them all together. With every story, we should ask these important questions: Who is the author? Who is this story all about? At times, did it appear that one of the lesser characters was the main character? What kind of journey are the characters going on? Is the journey easy or difficult for them? What purpose connects all the characters and the journey together? Why did the author pick these characters—both the main and lesser characters? Why this journey? Why connect these characters with the journey? Why give the story a purpose?

These are some important questions we can ask about every story that we read or watch. Not only are these valid questions to ponder for someone else's story, but you should also use them to examine the story of your own life. That's the main reason for asking these questions. Ask yourself who is the author of your life. Who is your story all about? Reflect on the journey you've taken so far and the purpose behind that journey.

Since every story has an author, who is the author of your story? Are you writing your own story, or is someone else writing it? You might think, "It's my life, so I should be the one writing it, right?" That's what we would naturally think. What happens then if things don't go your way and life unexpectedly hits you from the side? We or our loved ones may be hit with unexpected trials such as fatal car accidents, cancer, the death of a child at birth, suicide of someone close to us, or divorce of one's parents. You may have your own list of undesirable things like these, but it's true that we have no control over these things, and they always seem to hit us out of nowhere. If we were writing our own stories, I'm sure none of us would want any of these things to happen to us. Yet, they still do, and far more often than we'd like.

It would be crazy to think that everything that has happened in our lives is all by random chance. Therefore, we should come to grips with the idea that we may not be the one writing our story. More likely, someone else is writing your story and mine. What if that is true? Could the author be some random person, or maybe it's someone who is greater than you or me? If that person is putting together the details of our lives and has control over things we can't control, then that person must have power and authority over humanity and our day-to-day lives. That would obviously make that person someone greater than us because there's no way a regular person can have that kind of authority over other people.

Assuming that you agree with my reasoning thus far, it seems clear that we're not the author of our story. Is it possible that we're the main character in our life story? Your story is about your life, so why wouldn't you be the main character? Considering the evidence showing that we aren't in control and we aren't the author of our story, we look toward this mystery author and ask why? When pain arrives in our lives, we ask why the pain we're experiencing is happening. At this point, we honestly may not even care who the author is; instead, we're so focused on all the good and bad of our life that we're distracted and miss one of the most important things we could ever be a part of. We may miss the opportunity to get to know the author. However, if the author of our story is real, we need to ask, "Who is He?" We can say whatever we want about this author, but what can we meaningfully say if we don't even know Him? Interestingly, He uses the pain and hurts that we face each day to draw us to know Him.

I don't know where you're located as you read this book, but around here, someone with such a high caliber of importance and authority is almost always perceived as God. You may agree or you may not. For the time being, let's just call this mystery author God for the sake of giving Him a name. Names have a unique power. As soon as we hear the name of someone or something, we immediately have a preconceived idea about that person or thing. For example, when I shared the list of hurts life may bring us and stated that the author of our life story is God, certain thoughts and images probably came to mind for each of those things. Your reaction may have been positive, or it may have been negative. For now, let's temporarily put those thoughts aside and simply consider the possibility of God as that someone who's over our lives and writing our story.

So far, we have the mindset that God is the author and that you and I may be the main character of our story. Next, we should ask who the side characters are and how they matter to us as the main characters. Are they insignificant to us, or are they of great importance in our lives? Simply put, the "side characters" are the people in our lives— people who have shaped us into who we are today. Good or bad, we wouldn't be who we are without them. These side characters may include parents, kids, students, classmates, coaches, teachers, bullies, nannies, coworkers, bosses, pastors, and many others. Maybe you have someone else in your life that I didn't list, but it's true that all these people have shaped you in some way. Some of them have more immediate influence on us than others, but they're all important as their lives are intertwined with our journey. Consider that we were each born at a certain time in history and at a certain place in the world (Acts 17:26) and that we know the people that we know. We can ask all the what-ifs we want, but it won't make any difference. We are still living the same life before we even thought to ask the questions.

As we go on through the journey of our life, people will come across our path. The time they are there and the impacts they make are all unique. No matter how unique their presence is in our lives, their presence is vital to who we are. They don't control who we are, but they can affect who we become. We are human, and it is human nature to interact with others. It's one of our greatest desires as a person, that can't be denied. It's interesting; the journey we take shapes the people who will be in our life, and at the same time the people in our life will also shape the journey we'll take. One isn't overpowering the other.

Let's review the main points we've covered so far. God is writing our story, and the story is about our life, so it's believable that we're the main character in our story. As we live out our life, our journey unfolds, and the people in our lives get to play small but important roles within our stories. Now, one of the most difficult questions you can ask is, "What's the purpose?" What's the purpose of my life? What purpose connects the author, all the characters, and the journey of my story? Why are we here? Why am I alive and living the life I'm living? This is a difficult question to answer. However, wrestling with this question is one of the most important things we can do to reveal what we truly value in life. I've heard people say that they want to do well in high school so they can go to a good college and major in a field that will get them a job they enjoy that pays them a lot of money. Along the way, they hope they'll find Mr. or Miss Right, marry, start a family, live in a nice home, and raise their kids to be proper members of society. After a successful career, they want to retire with a bunch of money in the bank, so they can live the rest of their lives to the fullest doing what they enjoy most. Doesn't that sound great? Almost everyone I know desires this kind of life more than anything else. Don't get me wrong. Some of these things are great, but I wouldn't say they're my greatest desire, greatest pursuit or purpose of my life. When they are completely honest, people who pursue these things as their main purpose say that they still feel some emptiness in their hearts. They feel like something is missing. What can we do? If you feel that way, I assure you that you're not alone. I believe that most of the people you know have similar feelings, but they don't want to express them and let others know.

Is this really what my story is about? I believe the problem we have is a matter of perspective: We tend to think that our story is all about me. First, we thought we were the author of our own story, and then we believed that we were the main character. But let's consider another perspective. Yes, this may be the story of my life, but what if it isn't about me? What if I'm just a side character in my story? Earlier, when we talked about the role that other people play in our stories, we considered them to be side characters in our story. Does that mean they're the main character in their story while I'm just a side character? Are there multiple stories going on at once, or is there one bigger true story? Next, we'll look at another story that will completely change your perspective of your own story.

Chapter 2

What Is God's Story?

If there is only one true story, it would be God's story since He's God. He has that name for a reason. You wouldn't call someone God unless you truly believed everything about that person is greater and grander than anything and everything else. God has His own story just as we do, so to know how we're connected to Him, let's get to know Him a little bit more. How do we get to know someone we've never met—especially someone who has a reputation of being greater than anything and everything we could possibly understand? Fortunately, God has made information about himself easily accessible and available to us. Most people know it as the Bible, but I like to call it God's Word. Based on how His character lines up with the words in the Bible, I can tell that the Bible is His actual words to us.

When God Speaks

Some may be skeptical about God and His word for various reasons. If you are skeptical, I encourage you to consider this example. Have you seen The Hobbit and The Lord of the Rings trilogies? It's okay if you haven't; the example still works because the specifics in the movies aren't important; it's the scope of the movies that matters. These trilogies consist of six movies, and they are around three hours each; that's a total of around 18 hours of viewing time. That's a total of around 64,800 seconds. If you only watched 10 random seconds of those 18 hours/64,800 seconds and I asked you to tell me what all the movies are about, could you do it accurately? That would be a ridiculous request. You might say they had something to do with jewelry, weird creatures fighting, or another weird character desiring something that was precious to him. But you would miss the main point of the stories. That's exactly how so many of us view God's Word. We see a single line or a single Bible verse and we immediately have a preconceived thought, convinced that we know what God is saying. Maybe someone shared their opinion about Him, and we took their word for it without looking into His Word for ourselves. Instead of responding this way, I encourage you to look for the truth; desire and strive to find truth when you read or hear about God. You can only understand and appreciate the story of The Hobbit and The Lord of the Rings if you watch the movies or read the books in their entirety. Likewise, you can only understand, appreciate, and see the true story of the Bible, God's Word, if you read it for yourself and see what God is doing.

In the Bible, Acts 17:11 says, *"Now the Berean Jews were of more noble character than those in Thessalonica, for they received the message with great eagerness and examined the Scriptures every day to see if what Paul said was true."* Notice that these believers didn't just take Paul's word for the gospel; instead, they checked for themselves to verify that what he said was true. They didn't check once and never check it again, but they checked every day to make sure what was spoken to them matched up with the truth in God's Word. The Bereans weren't dishonoring the trustworthiness of Paul; they were giving honor and respect to the trustworthiness of God and His Word.

Who could possibly be the author of God's story? If the author is the person who has an overview of the story and knows every detail about what he's writing, who could write God's story besides God

Himself? It seems only logical to believe that God wrote His story, and since He's in it, He decided to write Himself into the story. No one else could tell us about the life of God except God Himself. The main difference between God as an author and human authors is that God had everything planned before He started writing; the rest of us make a plan as we write.

In 2 Timothy 3:16–17, the Bible says that *"All Scripture is God-breathed and is useful for teaching, rebuking, correcting and training in righteousness, so that the servant of God may be thoroughly equipped for every good work."* Thus, every word in the Bible is breathed out by God, and every word is His Word. As I said earlier, the words in the Bible are God's words to us. He's speaking and breathing out this story, and He's doing it for our benefit. The *"servant of God"* mentioned in this passage refers to someone who's living their life for God. Christians don't do good works to begin a relationship with God. Every Christian has a unique moment when they give their life to Him; then, out of that relationship, we do good works to help bring other people closer to Christ. Every word in the Bible is spoken by God, but He didn't physically write the words; humans did. You may ask how God can be the author if people are the writers.

The Hardest Worker

2 Peter 1:20–21 says, *"Above all, you must understand that no prophecy of Scripture came about by the prophet's own interpretation of things. For prophecy never had its origin in the human will, but prophets, though human, spoke from God as they were carried along by the Holy Spirit."* This means that humans spoke and wrote everything that's in God's Word, but they were carried along and held up by the Holy Spirit. The words didn't come from the human authors; they came from God.

Who is this Holy Spirit? He is extremely misunderstood, but

one thing that is sure is that He is God. I know this because of what it says in Acts 5:3–4 about when Peter (an apostle of Jesus Christ) accuses a husband and wife of lying to the Holy Spirit. Then, in Acts 5:4, he tells them, *"you have not lied to men but to God"* (NASB). They're accused of lying to the Holy Spirit and God, who are referenced as the same individual in this passage. Even though this couple had an unfortunate fate because of going against God, these verses clearly show that the Holy Spirit is the same person as God.

In John 14:26, Jesus says that the Holy Spirit is known as the Helper. In addition to constantly helping us, the Holy Spirit has other traits that we don't think about in terms of who He is and what He does. Here is a list of those traits quoted from *Theological Building Blocks for Biblical Counseling* by Dr. Nicolas Ellen:

I. The Person of the Holy Spirit:

A. The Holy Spirit has a mind/intellect (Romans 8:27).

B. He knows and searches the things of God (1 Corinthians 2:10–11, Isaiah 11:2, Ephesians 1:17).

C. He teaches people (1 Corinthians 2:12–13).

D. The Holy Spirit has emotions (Ephesians 4:30).

E. He is grieved by the sinful actions of people (Ephesians 4:30).

F. He is insulted when people reject the work of Christ (Hebrews 10:29).

G. The Holy Spirit has a will (Romans 8:2).

II. The Characteristics of the Holy Spirit:

A. The Holy Spirit is Omniscient (1 Corinthians 2:11–12).

B. The Holy Spirit is Omnipresent (Psalm 139:7).

C. The Holy Spirit is Omnipotent (Job 33:4).

D. The Holy Spirit is called Truth (1 John 5:6).

III. The Work of the Holy Spirit:

A. The Holy Spirit gives resurrection life (Romans 8:2, John 3:6).

B. The Holy Spirit sets believers apart (2 Thessalonians 2:13).

C. The Holy Spirit comforts believers (John 14:16).

D. The Holy Spirit gives life to creation (Job 27:3, 33:4, Psalm 104:30).

E. The Holy Spirit gave order to creation (Isaiah 40:12, Job 26:13).

F. The Holy Spirit is the divine author of Scripture (2 Peter 1:21).

G. The Holy Spirit was the agent of the virgin birth of Jesus Christ (Luke 1:35, Matthew 1:20).

H. The Holy Spirit raised Jesus from the dead (Romans 8:11, Romans 1:4).

I. The Holy Spirit indwells believers (John 14:16–17).

J. The Holy Spirit empowers believers to live a holy life (Ephesians 5:18).

K. The Holy Spirit restrains sin from going as far as it could go (2 Thessalonians 2:6–7).

L. The Holy Spirit empowers people to walk with Christlike character (Galatians 5:16–23).

M. The Holy Spirit joins us to Christ and His people (1 Corinthians 12:13).

N. The Holy Spirit seals believers in Christ (Ephesians 1:13).

O. The Holy Spirit teaches truth (John 14:26).

P. The Holy Spirit guides us into truth (John 16:12–15).

Q. The Holy Spirit helps believers to understand truth (1 Corinthians 2:10–16).

R. The Holy Spirit gives believers supernatural abilities to serve one another in the body of Christ (1 Corinthians 12:1–11, Hebrews 2:4).

S. The Holy Spirit convicts believers and unbelievers of sin (John 16:7–8).

T. The Holy Spirit performs miracles (Acts 8:39).

U. The Holy Spirit testifies or witnesses (John 15:26, Romans 8:16).

V. The Holy Spirit intercedes for us to God (Romans 8:26).

IV. Conclusions for the Believer:

A. Those who walk by the Holy Spirit will experience the life and peace that surpasses explanations or understanding (Romans 8:1–11).

B. We are to put to death ungodly thoughts, words, and actions through the power of the Holy Spirit so that we will live godly lives that please and honor God (Romans 8:12–13).

C. We are to walk by the Spirit, which is submitting your thoughts, motives, desires, words, actions, relational patterns, and service to the standards of Scripture as He empowers us to do so (Galatians 5:16–25). The more we walk by the power of the Holy Spirit, the more He will validate our adoption into the family of God (Romans 8:14–17).

The Holy Spirit is truly the hardest worker, constantly working for the glory of God in our lives. He's like that special person at church who is constantly working behind the scenes, but no one knows the amount of time and effort they're putting in caring for the rest of the church. As our short list showed, the Holy Spirit does many things for us, but one of His most important roles is that He enters our heart when we give our life to Christ. At that moment, we have two spirits living in us—our own human spirit with which we were born and God's Holy Spirit, which we receive when we give our life to Him. They don't ever have conflict unless we decide to turn our back against God and attempt to live life our own way. Inner turmoil in the Christian's heart is a result of trying to live that way. Also, one spirit won't ever forcefully overpower the other; God gives us the freedom to choose and make our own decisions while we live in His predestined plan. God desires harmony with us more than anything else, and we can only do that through His love. He desires a relationship and fellowship with us. He loves us and cares about us more than we could possibly understand. He wants us to love Him in that same way, but we can only do that through God's power. We are completely dependent on Him to enable us to live a righteous life.

Father Like Son

Jesus Christ is also known as God—usually called the Son of God. He and the Holy Spirit are not two separate gods, but the same One. A lot of Bible passages tell us that Jesus is also God. One such passage is in John 10:24–38. I won't quote it all here, but you should look it up for yourself, along with the rest of the verses I've mentioned. In summary, Jesus says that both He and the Father (God the Father) are one and the same. Not many people would make such a bold statement, especially in the religiously hostile part of the world where Jesus lived at that time. Even in these verses, the people He's talking with try to kill Him. The situation was dangerous because the Jews were a religious people living under the rule of a strict and harsh people, the Romans. The rulers of Israel were more fearful of the Romans than they were of the truth of God and His Word.

In John 10:24–38, Jesus tells them that He is God, just as God the Father is God. In verse 24, the Jews to whom he is speaking said to Him, *"If You are the Christ, tell us plainly"* (NASB). In verse 30, Jesus says, *"I and the Father are one"* (NASB). Most people, including myself, view God the Father as the One who led His people out of slavery from Egypt as recorded in the Bible's Old Testament. He was present with His people throughout biblical times.

The Holy Spirit, Jesus Christ, and God the Father are three separate persons who are all God. They aren't separate gods, but the same One. This God has been referred to as the three-in-one Godhead; their hearts, desires, and purposes are all unified as one. Two worship songs that describe God as three in one are "This I Believe (The Creed)" by Hillsong Worship and "How Great Is Our God" performed by Chris Tomlin. I mention that because many people find it easier to connect with words in a song than with words on a page.

He wouldn't be known as God if He wasn't greater than anything and everything we could possibly understand. His greatness is evident in the fact that He is three separate persons, but one God. Of course, I can't fully understand Him, and I'd be surprised if I met someone who thought they could. Are you content with not being able to place Him in a box or contain Him in the confines of your mind? I don't think anyone with the name God can be understood and contained on a human level. Not being able to prove or disprove His existence, we have to say that faith is a major factor. Faith is an essential part of our walk with Christ (Ephesians 2:8). By faith, we can accept that He is the Triune God, and now, it's His story that we'll be looking at.

Story Time with God

I think we have established that there is good reason to believe that God is the author of His own story. He breathed out everything in the Bible. As the Holy Spirit carried the human writers along from the beginning of time, He had them write what is known as the Bible, His Word. Now, we need to ask who God's story is all about. Who is the main character of His story?

When we looked at our own story, we initially thought that we were the main character in our story. In the same way, wouldn't God be the main character of His story? Yes and no. We must realize that nothing is more important than glorifying God; He is worthy of all praise and honor. So, yes, God is the main character in His story; in fact, God's story centers around one of the persons of the Godhead: Jesus Christ. When He lived as a human, He glorified God the Father above all else and lived for Him in every moment. Everything in God's story is about Jesus, the Son of God, and everything exists to bring us to Him.

Colossians 1:16–17 says, *"For in Him [Christ] all things were created: things in heaven and on earth, visible and invisible, whether thrones or powers or rulers or authorities; all things have been created through Him and for Him. He is before all things, and in Him all things hold together."*

From this Scripture, we can see that Christ is God; in Him everything was created; all things have been created through Him; He is before all things, and He holds everything together. When it says, *"in Him and through Him everything was created,"* that includes you, me, and everyone else we know. Every one of us is a unique individual—from the appearance of our body to the character of who we are deep inside. When it says, "everything has been created for Him," we understand that He is the centerpiece of all creation. As people who were created by Him, we are also supposed to glorify

God and live our lives for Him. Every bit of creation is for Him, no matter how big or small—from the most beautiful scenery to our own life to the grass and dirt we pass every day. It all exists and has purpose to glorify God.

He didn't just create us and say that everything is all about Him, so we should live for Him and do what He says with no questions asked. He cares about us and loves us. Now, when it says, "in Him all things hold together," it means that He is the glue that makes everything stick and hold together. When it says, *"hold together,"* I think of multiple broken pieces becoming whole again. Each one of us is a broken person being made whole again by Him. We are also collectively broken people who carry hurts almost every time we interact with others, but collectively, He is making us whole again as His body, the church.

When it comes to interacting with others, I'm terrible with friendships, but I know that when I interact with another Christian, we have at least one thing in common: Jesus Christ has come into our lives, and we belong to Him. In fact, I feel like Jesus Christ is the only thing that connects me with the people I know. Even if nothing else connects us, with Jesus I feel like I'm part of a family where I can call other Christians brothers and sisters in Christ.

As broken people, how can we be made whole? Jesus Christ is the only one who could possibly bring us that sort of healing. It only happens in our life through knowing who He is, what He cares about more than anything, and what He's done to fix our brokenness. Because He is God, He must have been there at the beginning when He said, *"'Let there be light'; and there was light"* (Gen. 1:3 NASB) and also when He said, *"Let Us make man in Our image"* (Gen. 1:26 NASB). A little over 2,000 years ago, Jesus decided to leave heaven and come to earth. He left perfection and entered imperfection. He went from being worshipped constantly to being denied, mocked, and rejected. He didn't come as a king or ruler of heaven but as a fragile little baby boy who could've easily died. Believe it or not, His mother was a virgin. It would've been impossible for her to have a child at that point if God had not made the impossible possible. Soon after Jesus was born, the local king, who was threatened by His birth, *"gave orders to kill all the boys in Bethlehem and its vicinity who were two years old and under"* (Matt. 2:16). Imagine the chaos all throughout the country. What if something like this happened in your town, city, county, state, or country? There are moments of brokenness like this one throughout the Bible, but God never does anything without a good reason and purpose behind it.

There's not much of Jesus's life recorded in the Gospels until He started His ministry at about age 30 and continued for the next three years. Those three years are filled with a lot of good things, mostly telling and showing the people around Him who He is and what He's all about. Jesus did many miracles, such as healing people, forgiving people's sins, reviving someone from the dead, removing demons, walking on water, and commanding nature to be quiet. His ministry climaxed with His death, resurrection, and ascension.

God is the only one who can speak to the deepest parts of another person's heart. That's the Holy Spirit at work. When is the last time you have done something miraculous like that? Of course, the answer is never. God is the only one who can do that. The only way we could even come close to doing that is through the Holy Spirit. The closer we are to God, the more we think like Him and do things like He does. I mean, the closest thing I've done is to speak words that are encouraging or inspiring in line with God's Word, but honestly, even that was all from God. He's speaking to others through me; I'm simply a messenger.

Since He can speak to a person's heart, take a moment and ask yourself what's the status of your heart? Have you thought of this before, or is this the first time? It's not something many people think about, but I dare say that this is one of the greatest questions we need to ask ourselves. By "status," I mean how alive is your heart? I know you're physically alive and that your heart is beating because you're reading this book, but let's think on a deeper and more spiritual level. We feel pain, love, or joy in our heart at times, but we are not referring to our physical heart. Rather, we are referring to who we are as a person—our soul and spirit. But we like to call it our heart because that's where it feels like it comes from within us. I know that some days, I feel more or less alive than others, so what is the deciding factor on how alive I feel? It depends on what we value. If Jesus Christ is the greatest thing we value, then we should be as alive as we can be that day, but if we shift our focus from Him onto other things, then our sense of being alive will be diminished that day. I constantly ask myself whether I'm valuing God above everything else. Even if I am, it won't completely determine how I feel. Even though He is my greatest value, my heart could be hurting and sorrowful about something else that has happened recently. I could be hurting and sorrowful but still have a peace from God because I am more content in Him than worried about my circumstances.

One of the things that makes Christianity different from all other religions is that Jesus isn't just a man; he is God—not half and half, but all in all. He's not 50 percent man and 50 percent God. He's 100 percent man and 100 percent God. He was in heaven, but He came down to earth and lived as a human, so we can completely relate to Him. The life He lived was perfect, but He died a horrific and unjust death. By the power of God, He was resurrected from the grave three days later. When He died, He took on all the sins of mankind because He was perfect. His perfection enabled Him to take on all the sins from people in the past, present, and future. On the cross, He became the sins of all time and was separated from His Father since sin can't exist in the presence of God. Keep in mind that sin always leads to pain, misery, and ultimately, death. Christ took on all the sins committed by every person from the past, present, and future. He became them all in a single moment. Then, as the embodiment of sins at that time, He died. Through His own death, He put to death all sins.

Every. Single. Sin. Is. Dead.

Including one we may be living in now.

Know this. Trust Him. Live for Him now.

If that were the end of God's story, it would feel like you had attended the funeral of an honorable person who had sacrificed much for so many, but that's not the end. Human stories usually end with death, but this is God we're talking about here. His story doesn't end with death. God is greater than anything and everything we could think or imagine, including death. Jesus was raised from the grave by the Holy Spirit, being separated from sin, and keeping sin in its proper place of death. Being the perfect God-man, in His resurrection, Jesus made an escape route for all of us in regard to sin. When He rose, He didn't remove all the wickedness in the world. We can tell that it's still here. We only need to take a quick look at the news. Sin still lives here, and the only way we can get rid of it in our own life is through Jesus Christ and believing who He is and what He's done for us. When we believe in Jesus, our life is slowly transformed from a sinful life to a righteous life in Christ.

What Jesus did for us was to give up His life for ours, and in doing so, He put to death all the sin in our life. We're able to see this exchange when He was hanging on the cross. At that point, all the sin we had committed was forgiven. Everything from the past, present, and future has all been forgiven. Even though He already forgave us, we need to ask Him for forgiveness. This moment is all about initiating a relationship with Him. Then, we should naturally desire to live our life for Christ, giving it all to Him.

Acts 16:31 says, *"They replied, 'Believe in the Lord Jesus, and you will be saved—you and your household.'"* Also, Romans 10:10 says, *"For it is with your heart that you believe and are justified, and it is with your mouth that you profess your faith and are saved."* Finally, 1 Corinthians 10:31 says, *"So whether you eat or drink or whatever you do, do it all for the glory of God."*

The Bible is God's story. It's centered around Jesus Christ; it's for us, but it's also for us to give to others, and in doing so, we give Him glory. The purpose of God's story is to bring us to Him and be closer to Him each day. That means we're the side characters of His story, not the main character. Our role will rarely seem significant, but it is. We have an opportunity to be in the same story as God by sharing Christ with others. The journey we're put on is different for each of us. Meeting Christ is the one thing we have in common. Getting to know someone may not always be a journey, but when it comes to Jesus Christ and God, I can promise you, it's a journey of a lifetime. It's the most unforgettable thing that will happen to you, and it's an everyday, every moment, lifetime kind of journey.

The characters in God's story are God and us. The "us" refers to everyone—past, present, and future. We're all the people in God's story. The purpose that connects everyone together in God's story is simply this: we are to glorify and worship God. The main way this happens is by connecting our own story with God's story. Since the purpose of His story is to connect our story with His, then it seems like we may not really understand what's going on in our story if we try to view it apart from God. How does God's story affect yours? Is your story not all about you? What is really going on in your story? If there's only one true story, then, what is the real story?

Chapter 3

What Is the Real Story?

How are we connected to God? In God's story and our story, we've identified the author, the main character, and the side characters; we've begun to understand the journey and the purpose that connects all these elements. Now, let's consider how our story and God's story are connected to each other. The only similarity is the author; everything else is different. The author for both stories is God. The main character in our story is us, but the main character in God's story is Jesus Christ. The side characters in our story is everyone around us, but the side characters in God's story is us. The journey in our story is intertwined with the side characters, in which they influence one another and shape one another. The journey that Jesus takes in God's story is also intertwined with the side characters, but the journey is only influencing and shaping the side characters in the story, not the other way around. Finally, the purpose of our story is all about us. The purpose in God's story is all about Jesus Christ—it is about his sacrifice for us and ultimately glorifying Himself through us. The purpose of His story is to connect us with Him, so He connects our story with His story. If He does that, doesn't that mean there's only one story? How does this even work? What happens to our story then?

God doesn't eliminate our story. That's not how God works. The life we lived and our past still exist in our memories. Our story is completely intact, but so is God's story. In fact, our story becomes part of God's story. Initially, we tend to think that our story is all about us, but gradually, we realize we're part of something far bigger than us. That far bigger thing is God's story. How and when we come to that realization will be different for each of us; that time may be referred to as the day we give our life to Christ. Unfortunately, some people won't make it to that day, and that's the worst thing that could ever happen to them. It's my hope that's not the case for you or anyone else you know. Jesus Christ is always the game changer for our story; the moment we meet Him is the moment our story starts to get good. Knowing Christ is the climax of the story or the pivotal scene in our story changes everything for the better.

If He makes everything better, what was wrong in the first place? Why do we need Him to come into our lives? Sin is the reason. I don't know what you've heard about sin or what comes to mind when you hear the word *sin*. Most people seem to view sin as a label for doing something wrong, but it goes much deeper than that. In its simplest form, sin is anything we think, say, or do that's against who God is and what He's all about. Then, you may ask, what exactly is He all about? We only know who He is and what He's about because He tells us in His Word. If we read His Word, we'll start to understand Him, what He cares about, and the dangers of sin. If we live in line with His Word, we're living righteously, but if we live outside His Word, we're living in sin.

To start to understand sin, it helps to consider when sin entered the world for the first time. Sin began with Adam and Eve, the first man and woman. If you're unfamiliar with them, I encourage you to look at what the Bible says about them in Chapters 1–3 of Genesis, the first book in the Bible. God told them not to eat the fruit from a certain tree, but they did. In that moment, they sinned. What do you think was their sin? The sin wasn't eating the fruit as you might think, but it was disobeying God. It's about their relationship with God, not the fruit. Every time we sin, it has something to do with our relationship with God. Of course, we can sin against other people, but even then, we are sinning against God because He wants us to love others. No matter whether it's a sin against another person or God, it will always be something that keeps us from God. That's the essence of sin.

Love is the opposite of sin, so when we do not love God or others, we're living in sin. When we care for and love others, it's the same as loving God. He really does care about us and love us. The way God views us has to do with His heart for you and me. He knows and sees the dangers of the sins in which we're entangled. Not only does He know about our sin, but He consistently does something about it. Every time we're about to sin or in the middle of sinning, He gives us a way out, a way to make ourselves right with Him.

Instead of taking that opportunity to make their relationship right with God, Adam and Eve fled from Him, hiding and making excuses. When we're in the trenches of sin, we do the same thing. We try to hide behind excuses and attempt to justify what we did. Our specific sins may be different, but they're part of the real story of our lives. Stop fleeing, turn to God, and let's make ourselves right with Him. We need to let ourselves be loved. He's waiting with open arms.

Thanks to Jesus Christ, He killed sin once and for all on the cross. He buried all the sin in our lives by becoming sin when He died. Then, He beat death by rising from the grave on the third day. For those of us who believe in the resurrection of Jesus Christ, when we sin, we're living in the memories of our sin, completely forgetting about what Christ has done for us. Our eyes and hearts need to be consistently focused on Jesus. We need to be aware of our life of sin but be devoted to a new life with Christ. When we live for Christ, it's as if our life of sin is completely dead to us. We need to not only avoid sin but also be in the presence of Jesus Christ. Sin can't be in the same place as Christ, so we need to be in His presence. Living for

Christ means Christ lives in us. Once Christ is living in us, we have no room for sin to live in us. We need our eyes and hearts focused on Him. We need to ask ourselves the question: "Now that I have committed to follow Christ, how am I actually living for Him?" We should strive to live totally committed to Christ above all else. By becoming sin on the cross, He became our sin. By doing so, He permanently put to death any and all sin that we've participated in. I may sound repetitive, but that is intentional because it should be the song that continues to play in our hearts. Every thought and desire of our hearts should be focused on living for Him. Now, if we said that we'll live for Him, let's do it and live for Him.

How do we get there? How can Jesus be the light that lights our path (Psalm 119:105)? How can He be our greatest desire? How can He be the song that's repeating in our hearts? I just asked, "How do we get there?" The better question to ask is how does God let us get there? Because it's impossible to reach Him by our own abilities and power. We must rely on Him to reveal Himself to us in some way. Most of the time, when God is revealed to us, it is through someone sharing God's Word with us. Once we see who He is and what He's done for us, it becomes our responsibility to respond, and hopefully, we will give a positive response. The first step is simple. Truly believe in your heart that he died for you, taking the place of all your sins. Then, speak it out to Him. Tell Him that you want to give all your sins to Him and then start living for Him with all that you are. It's a bold thing to say you want to live that way, so when you do, mean it; truly mean it in your heart. This is the real story of our lives. We were living in sin, and Jesus took us out of it. Remember that Jesus Christ is and always will be the center of God's story. The real story of our lives begins when our story becomes intertwined with God's story. I hope you're able to see this become a reality in your story one day, if it hasn't happened yet.

What's next? To summarize, from the moment we put our faith

in Christ, the rest of our lives is simply about living for Christ. How do we do that? If He's your greatest desire, what will that look like in your life? There's no ABC manual that teaches us everything we need to know. There's the Bible, God's Word. That's a good place to start; actually, it's the best place to start. The Bible tells us a lot of things we should and shouldn't do, but there are also a lot of gray areas that aren't talked about as well. We need to rely on our relationship with God and His wisdom in those areas. There's also the church and everything it entails. We need to be involved in a good Bible-based church. The community of believers is always a huge help in these gray areas. When I say a Bible-based church, I'm talking about one that not only shares Scripture on Sundays to support the topic that the preacher is talking about, but also one that has its values deeply rooted in God's character and His Word.

At this point, the main thing to be done is for each of us to share our story. Telling others about when we met Christ is one of the best and most loving things we can do for Christ and those around us.

Part 2
My Testimony

Chapter 4

What's Your Heart behind What You Do?

Each day, we make different choices. Everything we do has a reason behind it. It's our heart behind what we do. Let's look at someone's job for example. They have their job for a certain reason. The purpose behind their job may be to earn money for themselves or their family. Most people need income to buy food and pay the bills to survive. They may have a different and even more personal reason outside of money or provision. For a few people, the job they have isn't the most important thing they do. This is so they can invest their time and energy into something else that they care about more, while they fulfill the necessity to pay their bills.

That's what I've done with most of the jobs I've had. My main priority is student ministry, so I've carefully chosen the types of jobs that can be molded around my time in student ministry when I'm focusing on bringing the students around me closer to Christ. The main point is this; in everything you do, you should have a reason for the decisions you make. We all make choices every day, but do you know the reason behind every choice you make? What's driving your choices?

My heart behind everything in this book is my story. In fact, it wasn't in my original plan to share anything else. Our story is the best tool in our arsenal to help bring others closer to God. It's a personal experience that connects our heart with God's heart. Even though my story is about me, it's ultimately all about Jesus Christ.

No matter what your story is about, He is the ultimate attraction in your story. I may be the one sharing my story, but God is the one who is constantly working in the hearts of those listening to it.

When I gave my life to Christ at age 17, all I wanted to do was simply follow Him and live for Him. I didn't care how it looked; I just wanted it. I wanted to give Him my all. I want to give God the glory above all else. God has shaped me in this journey, and I'm thankful for every moment of it. No matter how great or how awful it may seem at first glance, I wouldn't trade anything for it. Keep in mind that no matter what's in your story, God can use it to bring people to Him. One of the greatest things that has brought me close to God was learning how He shaped my story, and how He desired to connect it with His story.

Throughout my Christian life, I've had people tell me that God was going to use my story in a mighty way. Most of the time, this came from students since I was always around them. I got saved as a student and have continued to serve in student ministry since then. I've had a few adults tell me this as well, but there was a unique moment about six months before I started to write my story for this book. I was on a church trip in Israel, and each one of us got baptized in the Jordan River. When someone gets baptized at church, they share their faith story, so before we got baptized in the Jordan River, we each shared our own testimony. It was a public place where many people come to get baptized, and I was one of the last ones in our church group. Another group was gathering to use our location after us, and they heard me share my story, so when I got out of the water, one of the guys approached me. He was a black guy with an unfamiliar accent, and he told me I was going to travel across the world, sharing my testimony, raising people from death to life. My immediate thought was, "Yeah right. I've heard that thousands of times, there's no way that's going to happen." Even though I thought that, God was already deeply pressing on my heart to get my testimony out in public. He gave me a deep longing to share it, whenever the opportunity arose. The problem was that for years, I had an internal conflict of wanting to share my story but believing that it would never happen.

About six months before my trip to Israel, I shared my story through an online website and at church on video. The website is stories.church; check it out if you are interested in hearing people's stories and what God has done in their lives. I didn't really like myself in my own story video, so I wasn't satisfied and wanted to do something more to get my story out.

When I got home from our Israel trip, I had the line that guy said stuck in my head, "...sharing your testimony, raising people from death to life." I only thought about this raising from death to life in a spiritual sense. I rarely went out with people, so I had plenty of alone time with God. During that time, I prayed and thought about what God would want, seeking to understand whether what that guy said was true and how I would approach getting my story out. It was a constant struggle in my mind. I decided to continue my normal routine going to work and school and serving in church. I tried to continue living for Him and prayed for His plan to unfold in my life. It felt like forever, but after six months, I decided to take some action and go with what I felt was God's plan; I became convinced that writing my story in a book was the route God wanted me to take.

Chapter 5

In the Beginning

My story began 29 years ago, and the beginning wasn't at all peaceful. Looking at my life now, you wouldn't guess I had issues at my birth, but I learned that I wasn't expected to survive my mother's pregnancy. On top of that, I was an extremely unhealthy newborn. When I was born, the doctors performed two tests—at one minute and another at five minutes after I was born. The tests show how healthy the baby is based on a scale from 0 to 2 in five different areas making a total score of 0 to 10. I didn't even get anything on the first test, and on the second one, I only got a 2 or a 3. I couldn't breathe on my own, so they hooked me up to some sort of oxygen machine. Later that day, they transported me to another hospital that specialized in treating my medical condition. This was all happening in 1990 when all things medical and technological were not as sophisticated as they are now.

I was at the new hospital for the next two weeks until I could be taken home. I had a few problems during that short time. The first and the most memorable one for my parents is that one of the nurses burned my leg by spilling some sort of chemical right above my ankle. If it had hit my ankle, it would've paralyzed that leg; I have a scar where it burned through the skin. That's why I can call it memorable; it's like a tiny mark seared on my body as a reminder of everything God did for me when I was born.

I was also very weak, and my body was limp. Because of that, there was a high possibility I might have cerebral palsy, which I've been told is when you have a very small amount of muscle and very little muscular control. However, over the next couple weeks of life, I was seen by a therapist, and it turned out that I was physically normal like any other child.

During those two weeks in the hospital I had a unique moment that I could easily visualize later in my life. The best way I can describe it is that it was an out-of-body experience. I'll go into more detail about that part of my story at a more appropriate time. From the time I found out about it, this moment has been a reaffirmation of God's love, even when it felt like I was all alone against the world. Unfortunately, I had a lot more of those lonely moments growing up than there should be for a kid.

After making it home from the hospital, my parents had a therapist come to the house several times a week to do checkups to see how I was doing. According to my parents, on the doctor's first visit, he had a surprised look and said these exact words, "Babies like this, they just don't make it." Even though I survived physically, both the doctor and therapist were cautious and expected me to be mentally slower than the average kid. Later, they suggested that I be placed in a special education class, so when school started, that's where I was for part of my school day.

Around the time school started, I had another incident where I hurt myself. We had a fishbowl with a goldfish in it on top of my dresser. I decided I wanted to see it up close, so I pulled out all the drawers and started climbing on up. As I was getting to the top, the dresser fell with me, shattering the fishbowl right next to me. My mom rushed in the room and saw me bleeding as I sat next to the dresser, not crying or anything. Believe it or not, the only thing that happened was that my hand was cut by a piece of glass. Given the way I was climbing, I think I should've been crushed by the dresser, but, for whatever reason, I ended up next to it after it fell. When we got the cut taken care of, the doctor said that if it had been any deeper, it could've cut the nerves in my hand and permanently paralyzed it. That was another close call that could've affected how I would live the rest of my life. Can you look at your own life and see moments like this? Is there anything that happened in your life that could've been far worse than it was? Be grateful for these moments that didn't turn out as bad as they could have.

On a different and more spiritual note, I was aware of God at an early age. Shortly after I started talking, I was playing an original, old-school, brick-sized Game Boy. One day, I was riding in an elevator with my mom while I was playing my Game Boy. I suddenly stopped and said as best a kid could say, "You know, God must be the very best video game player." Then, I continued playing. It was a completely random kid moment, but it revealed how I viewed God, even though I didn't truly know Him yet. I thought that whatever He did, He would be the best at it. As a kid I knew of Him, but I didn't personally know Him yet. How do you view Him? Do you personally know Him from the time you spend with Him in His Word and prayer, or do you just know of Him from what you've heard from someone else?

When I started school, I was first put in an interfaith class before moving on to preschool. I then went into the normal grade school plan starting in kindergarten until I graduated high school. At each place, the other kids and adults treated me like I was special or different, and it was almost never a good special or different. When I started kindergarten, it was obvious because I spent half my day in a regular class with regular kids; then, I was taken to the special education class for the other half of my school day. While I was in that class the material was super easy and fun. I enjoyed it, because I always finished early and was able to help the other kids in my class. Oddly enough, I had this natural compassion and consideration for others—to think of them before myself. Despite this, I was still viewed as "special" and "different" by the regular kids, and I was often teased and made fun of. I left the special education class halfway through my second grade year, but I was still treated the same. The only difference in my life was that since I wasn't in the special education class anymore, I couldn't be there for the kids whom I helped, which was one of the most hurtful things I felt at that time.

The teasing and poor treatment continued and even escalated over time. It didn't matter whether I was at school or my church's Sunday school. The building doesn't ever make the difference; it always depends on the people, and it doesn't matter the age. The way people treat others comes from their hearts. We each have desires and values, and they will be the guide for how we act. We may desire to be valued by others or try to convince ourselves that we have value, so we'll treat some people a certain way. Most people will put down others, so they can feel lifted up. In doing this, we attempt to fill up that value and desire in our heart, but the end of that pursuit is never satisfied. This is true for all of us, whatever stage of life we may be in. If we ever want a satisfied desire or value in life, we can't try to get it from ourselves. It must come from God. He is the only one who can satisfy our souls.

Chapter 6

Day-to-Day Survival

When I was eight years old, I transitioned out of my special education class. Six months later, we stopped going to church. By that time, I was so fed up with how I was being treated that I tried to hang myself one night. I constantly felt alone, like no one loved or cared about me. No matter what I did that night in attempting to hang myself, it didn't work. All I could do was cry myself to sleep because of how miserable I felt. I had many more nights like that, but I've never made such an obvious attempt on my life after that. Even though Job never tried to take his own life, I truly felt the kind of desperation that he expresses in Job Chapter 3, mainly verses 11, 16, 20–24, and 26.

Throughout my life, I've thought of countless scenarios where I could've died in some way. The feelings of these experiences increased more and more over time. I tried to become more discreet and sneakier in my attempts. Almost every night, I would try to go out for a bike ride or a walk. I would intentionally wear dark clothes, not caring whether people could see me. If something had happened, it would've been because I was trying to set myself up so that it would seem like an "accident."

Looking back at all those nights, they were times when I had some of the best one-on-one talks I've ever had with God. I know that's weird to hear, but every time I went out, I would vent my frustrations. As I talked, I always felt some sort of response within my heart. Sometimes, I would feel a strange peace, but other times, I was left with the same intense feelings of loneliness. During many of those late nights, I even prayed for God to kill me or end my life in some way. I didn't care. I wanted to stop living, breathing, or even feeling; these feelings stayed with me for many years.

I was 11 years old and in sixth grade when I started going to church again with my mom. At first, my dad didn't have any interest in going to church, but he started coming a couple weeks after we did. He came little by little; then he started to come more consistently. I mention him, not because he had a massive impact in my story, but I believe it's important to know the spiritual position of a student's parents to know what kind of spiritual environment the student grew up in.

I didn't want to go to youth church because of my previous experience with church and being around other kids my age. That summer, I went to my first church camp, and it was the first time that I remember being asked to give my life to Christ. I was 12 at the time. During one of the sermons later in the week, they did the church camp thing where they ask you to raise your hand if you want to be saved. I was sitting in the back to avoid people as much as I could. I noticed that a lot of kids raised their hands, so I decided to as well. That was me following the crowd rather than Jesus. In that moment, I still knew of God, but I didn't personally know Him yet, and I didn't have any desire to get to know Him any more than I did already. I saw church as just another activity that my parents had me involved in that I would have to try to survive.

At first, I didn't go to youth group regularly; I stayed with my mom at "big church" most weekends. The youth did worship music and teaching, but everything seemed to be more fun-focused than anything else. From the silly and ridiculous games to all the goofy videos I saw when I went, there were many things to temporarily distract me from my real-world problems each week.

I encourage youth pastors and leaders to know their students. It's possible that students could be using some of your activities as a temporary distraction to hide from their pain instead of addressing the heart of the issue. That's what happened in my life. We all need to be intentional, showing students the love they need; however, avoiding the heart issues won't make their pain go away. We need to go after their real issues and free our students from the things that are enslaving them, so they can finally be free to live for Christ.

When it was time to transition into seventh grade church, I refused to go and begged my mom not to make me go. I knew things wouldn't go well with the other students. She made me go anyway, and just like I thought, I had problems the very first weekend there. Right after worship when I was about to sit down, one of the kids behind me pulled my chair right out from under me, and I fell to the floor. Honestly, if this had been something that only happened once, it wouldn't have been that big of a deal. I could have shrugged it off like I had done in the past, but things like this happened to me more frequently after I was eight years old.

When you interact with someone, you don't know what their life has been like before that moment. They could've had 99 negative interactions, and what you say or do to them could be the 100th one that ends up drowning them in their sorrow. On the other hand, your positive and encouraging interaction could cancel out the 99 negative ones. Your interaction with them could be the one that has the biggest impact on their life, for better or for worse.

Within the next year, my parents started helping at church each weekend. Since they were serving at each worship service, I would usually be one of the first and last students there each weekend. Ours was a large church with three services—one on Saturday and two on Sunday—so, I was there for a lot of time. Every weekend before and after church, I would go to the corner of our large student game room where there weren't many people and immerse myself in video games. When one of the pastors noticed that I was one of the last ones each week, he asked me if I could help put away various items and close down everything in the game room. This happened when I was 13, during my eighth grade year.

Because I had a willing heart to help others, I decided to help. I'm not some super Christian; I was there and the need for help was expressed, so I did. Since I was always there, it made it easier for them to ask for my help with other things over time. I'd help with small insignificant tasks such as moving chairs or picking up the trash other students left, but I enjoyed helping and doing something for someone else. My help, week in and week out, started to make the other pastors and other students view me as a leader in our student ministry. I wasn't living spiritually or anything like that. I believe everyone started to view me that way only because of my consistent involvement. They started to view me as a leader, but I didn't ask for that. Nor did I even want it.

Even though I was seen as a leader, I still had this deep, aching misery in my heart every day. The other students thought highly of me, but deep in my heart, I still wanted to die every day I lived. I wasn't willing to try to kill myself, but I felt so miserable that I did want to die. My heart constantly felt empty and dead inside. I was surrounded by people, but I always felt alone. I appeared to be okay, but I never was; I faked it every time I was at church or around church people. I was no longer real with people. I did this so much that I forgot what it was like to be real. For me, being fake became the new real. I lived like this from 8th to 11th grade—from 13 to the time I gave my life to Christ when I was 17.

I hope that church and youth leaders can see that because I gave the appearance of being good, many others viewed me as a spiritual leader in the church. I served all over the church because I saw that help was needed, and no one else was stepping up and doing it. So, I was viewed this way not only from students, but also by adults throughout my church. The reality of the situation was that I truly wasn't in a good place with God because I didn't personally know Him yet. I was simply trying to survive, and this was one of the best ways for me to fit in. As a student ministry leader, if you've trusted students to be leaders in your youth ministry, ask yourself whether they are truly in a good place with God, or are they making an appearance like I was. God's Word is your only trustworthy guide in discerning that; watch their heart, like God looks at the heart.

Between ages 14 and 17, which were my 9th through 11th grade years, before I gave my life to Christ, I tried being open about my pain twice. I shared it with people around my age whom I thought I could trust. Both times their response was all about trying to fix what I presented them; that brought more negative conflict into my life. One of the people I shared it with, shared it with my parents, and they tried to apply their own solutions as well. They made me do counseling, and the therapists suggested that I take medicine for depression. I boldly refused them and never had any. I was stubborn when it came to the counseling; I didn't care for it whatsoever or try to apply it to my life.

I believe that we should be counseled when we need it, but the Bible should be the source, not the support. After all, one of the Holy Spirit's names is The Counselor (John 14:26 CSB, 16:13, 1 Corinthians 2:10–16). Since He guided everything that's in God's Word (2 Peter 1:21), and He lives in our heart once we give our life to Christ (Ephesians 1:13), there can be no greater counselor in our life than God and His Word. Even though He's our greatest counselor, He shouldn't be our only counselor. We need to surround ourselves with people who highly value God and His Word. This is something I did not do during my adolescent years, but I wasn't following Christ at the time, so I didn't know better.

Before I gave my life to Christ, I didn't trust anyone else with the turmoil that was going on in my heart. Even after I gave my life to Christ, I was still cautious with whom I shared my story. When I was open and shared what was going on in my life, all I wanted was someone to simply care.

Chapter 7

The Heart of Summer

I finally gave my life to Christ toward the end of summer in 2007 when I was 17. When I say, "I gave my life to Christ" or when you hear someone else say that, you should understand how deep of a meaning those words have. As I write those words now, I truly mean that I gave my life to Christ; that is, I made a promise to commit every ounce of my life to live for Him. That's what I mean and that's what we should mean when we make our faith commitment. Every time God spoke, His words were 100 percent trustworthy and full of truth. He wanted the same from the relationship He had with His people. God's Word is the greatest thing He gave to let us know the truth in His heart. Nothing else matters in comparison to Him.

I may fail daily since I'm a human with a sinful heart, but I have this desire to live completely for Him. Christ simply means Savior, so once we accept that He saved us from the destruction of our sin, why wouldn't we want to give our life to Him? The Holy Spirit, who dwells in the saved person's heart, is the only one who can give us the desire to live for God. When we say that we give our life to Christ, we must not be halfway in. When you decide to give anything (money, time, or whatever), you either give or you don't. So, when we say we're a Christian living for Christ, let's not only say it, but live it out (James 1:22–25).

Let's head back to my story at the beginning of summer 2007. I had just finished my junior year in high school. Looking back, I can see that God did a whole lot in my life that summer. The first thing that God used to speak to me was an evening youth event with a guest speaker, Nick Vujicic (voy-check), who had been born without arms or legs. He had a comedic personality along with an inspirational story even though he had experienced pain throughout his life because of how others treated him. Despite the pain and disability, he was able to live his life in joy. The way I saw it, he was able to use his pain, controlling it, by turning it into joy.

Since he was born the way he was, he had to use a wheelchair to get around. Throughout his childhood, people made fun of him just because he was different. One day, he got so fed up with it that he was ready to end his life. He was so used to being hurt by others that he was shocked when a girl at school gave him a little word of encouragement. That tiny bit of encouragement made his day. This made me realize that you never know what your words will do. They could be words that push someone over the edge to end their life, or they could be words that make their day and help save their life.

That night, I realized that all the hurt and pain I had experienced could be the greatest tool in my arsenal to help others just as it was for Nick. Even though I was helping others, I still didn't consider Christ my greatest desire yet. I wasn't trying to live for Christ; I was just trying to be a nice person, which are two completely different things. I was simply going through the motions of life while doing some good things every now and then. Those good things have absolutely no benefit in earning us salvation or a relationship with Jesus Christ.

The next big event that summer was the student ministry summer camp at a beach in Florida. Nothing spectacular happened in my heart on that trip. I was so used to the normal summer camp routine from the fun games on the beach, to the upbeat worship music, to the guest speaker who set himself up during the week to share the typical salvation message on the last day. I had the process all figured out.

My problem was that I had it all in my head, but none of it was in my heart. I knew what the normal church routine was all about, but I had no idea what Jesus Christ was all about. It's crazy to say that although Christ is supposed to be seen in and through the church, I was oblivious to the miraculous power of Christ. It's possible to live every day in the place where Christ is supposed to be worshipped, but completely miss Him while we're there. I know I did that for many years and still do sometimes when I let sin reign in my heart rather than the Holy Spirit. Unfortunately, too many American Christians are missing out on Christ today: Christians don't need to just go to church; they need to actually live like the church. They need to be all in with their heart for God, His Word, and the gospel, which He wants us to share with others.

Some of the best moments of that summer camp week happened at the start of each day. Without any alarm, my body would naturally wake up between five and six o'clock each morning. It's just how I was wired. Every day, I would get up before anyone else, leaders included. I would go down to the very edge of the water where it was splashing onto the sand. As I sat there in silence with the sounds of the sea each morning, it would be dark, slowly getting brighter as the sun rose. Those moments were just me and God, and there was nothing better. It reminded me of the many late-night bike rides I had with God when I was younger, but there were no distractions with God on the beach, and it was the most complete and purest form of peace I have ever felt.

Now, I don't exactly remember what the sermons were about at that camp, but each year our student ministry had a summer theme. That year, the theme was Verge. As in, "God is on the verge of doing something great in your life." That was the main idea they kept speaking at us that summer. The description they gave us of verge is that something is right on the edge of happening. Without my knowledge, God was on the verge of doing something in my life that summer.

God doesn't waste a single moment. He was setting the mood and preparing my heart for when I would eventually give my life to Him. Right now, He could be in the process of preparing your heart for that glorious day when you will give your life to Him or the day you will come back to Him.

At this time, I wasn't aware that my birth had been a miracle, but my very life was on the verge of existence when I was born. The word *existence* fits perfectly because I wasn't even supposed to make it past the first trimester of the pregnancy. If I had died during pregnancy, the very thought of my life wouldn't exist except for a few people close to my parents. That would have been the life I lived but wouldn't have been the existence of my life. The moment we start to exist is the moment that God knows us, and from that moment on, He pursues us and wants us to know Him. He knows us far earlier and far later than anyone else possibly could.

It's crazy to think that every interaction I've had with others wouldn't have existed—for better or for worse. I would never have met or cared about the people I have known in my life; there would be nothing there. The past 12 years of investing in youth at the different student ministries I've been a part of would not have happened if I have not been born. Even this book wouldn't have been written.

God kept me alive for a reason, and He has kept you alive for a reason. Even if you feel like everyone is against you, know that God cares about you and loves you. Think about it. God has us all here for a reason, and everything He has given us is for a reason. Every person in your life has shaped you in some way, good or bad. They were also shaped by others and so on. God never wastes a moment, whether moments of blessings or moments of hardships. God has given them to us. So, don't waste your blessings or your hard times. The story we're living isn't only about you or me, but we're all part of a greater story. This greater story is God's story, and He's constantly on the verge of doing something greater in your life. We simply need to be open to Him.

The next big summer event in 2007 happened one week after camp. It was my first mission trip. Leading up to it, we were taught how to share our testimony. We had to write our testimony; that was the first time I had ever tried to do that. The first thing I thought was that I have never done drugs, had sex, or been drunk, so I must have the worst testimony ever. Oh boy, was I wrong. I learned that in our testimony, people want to hear about specific instances when we have faced pain or adversity and experienced some sort of overcoming power over our situation. Even if that's not part of someone's story, every testimony has the potential to be great. A truly great testimony reminds us that we were dead in our sin, that God came to us and completely cleansed us from the filth and death of sin, and that He made us alive in Him. No matter what cards are dealt to us in life, every great testimony ends at Jesus Christ, with us bowing down at His feet.

Our mission trip was just across the border into Mexico, but it was more than enough to open my eyes and heart to the reality of conditions in the world compared to the wealthy and healthy lifestyle I was raised in. Our main goals were serving the local kids by putting on soccer games for them, serving at a special-needs orphanage, and doing an activity within our group called EP letters.

The term *EP letters* stands for encouragement partner letters. At the end of each day, we would receive a letter without knowing who wrote it. We made it more fun by trying to figure who our partner was before they revealed themselves to us on the last day. As the week went on, it was a well-needed encouragement for me each day.

I was used to constant negativity, so some positive reinforcement was much needed for my soul.

For the soccer camps, we provided all the goals, nets, jerseys, and soccer balls, and when we left, we gave all the equipment to the local kids. The soccer camps were tons of fun even though the kids beat us every time despite being half our age and size. Only two people from our group could speak Spanish, but our facial expressions acted as a universal language. The local kids seemed so content even though they barely had anything. Their smiles spoke far more than any words could say. That was the first time I've ever seen that kind of contentment. The best way I could put it is that they had almost nothing, but they also had everything they needed. I believe that this "everything" they had was Jesus Christ.

The last thing we did was to help at a special-needs orphanage. When we arrived, I felt both uncomfortable and comfortable at the same time. In all honesty, I was not comfortable being around these kids because I hadn't been around kids like them since I left my class in second grade; I was uncomfortable because they were different from the people I usually spent time with. Yes, it was very hypocritical and sinful of me to think that way. At the same time, I felt comfortable because as I was with these kids, I felt strangely connected to them. It was as if I knew in the back of my mind and in my heart that I could have been in a similar situation even though I was not yet aware of what happened at my birth. While we were there, we simply fed them, played with them, and spent time with them. Over the whole summer, I probably did the very least here, but it's where God moved the most in my heart.

As soon as I got home from the mission trip, I asked my mom, "What happened to me when I was born?" I was firmly convinced in my heart that something unusual had happened, but I had no idea what it was. She tried to explain, but at that time I wasn't understanding what she was saying. I had one more week till my last trip scheduled for that summer, so I continually pestered my mom about it. She finally typed out something for me the night before I left. Our final trip that summer was divided between a student leadership conference in Washington, DC, and a mission trip in Baltimore, Maryland.

I didn't read what she typed till the last night of the conference. From that point on, I became aware that some sort of miracle happened at my birth. I knew I wasn't supposed to make it, but I did. Even though I didn't want to be alive, God wanted me alive. He has each of us here for a reason. That really struck my heart, and I thought, "Since God still has me around, why don't I make the most of it?"

God put the breath in my lungs, and He has every right to take it away at any moment He desires. The Bible says not to murder, and that also includes not murdering ourselves. He has authority over life and death, and if I were to take my own life, that would be denying the authority He has over my life. I would be rejecting Him in that moment, and I believe that's one of the most dangerous things we can do. We reject Him a lot every day, but we have opportunities to reconcile with Him. If I rejected Him by taking my own life, I would no longer be alive to seek reconciliation.

I've been asked many times whether someone who kills themselves is going to heaven. When we give our life to Christ, is the main goal of that decision to reach heaven, or is it to have a relationship with God? As the people of God, our greatest desire should be to glorify Him, not to reach a place. Everything we do should be all about living for Christ, and that includes the moment we give our life to Him. Murder and suicide don't have enough power to overpower the righteous glory of God and the ultimate redemptive work He did on the cross and being raised from the grave by the Holy Spirit three days later. The thoughts and actions of hate, murder, and suicide are simple, little sins in comparison to

God's power. All we need to do is simply confess to Him with our mouth that He's Lord and believe in our heart what He did, then we'll be saved (Romans 10:9).

So, did the people who took their own lives give their lives to Christ? The answer to that question is the same whether they're in heaven or not. Ultimately, only God and that person know whether they are saved, but we can tell by the evidence in a person's life and by the Holy Spirit working in their life. However, if they've taken their own life, it's almost impossible to know, so we can only have a hopeful faith that they were saved. If that's the case, it's never good to dwell on it, but it's also important that we don't waste the hardship of losing someone close to us. It's not beneficial to worry about something we don't have any power over, but God can grow us through it. I know this isn't the answer people are looking for in this situation, but it's the best answer that we can get. It puts us in a position where we absolutely must put our trust and faith in God. He doesn't waste a single moment. Let's live like Him and not waste one either, glorifying Him with every moment He's given us—good or bad.

Now, back to where I left off in my testimony. The second half of my last summer trip was a mission trip to Baltimore. We didn't do anything out of the ordinary. I felt like everything we did there, we could've done here as well. We did soccer camps in a field by the church where we were staying, and we did VBS at some of the local parks. At the end of the week, we ran a little festival for the community near the church. In each little thing we did, I simply wanted to give it all to God and live for Him and serve Him with all that I could. My mind and heart were solely focused on Him and nothing else.

Each night, we came together and discussed how our day had gone in the areas where we served. Even though I felt like I didn't do anything above and beyond at that time, toward the beginning of our discussion time, our pastor praised me in front of our group. He said that I had experienced rapid spiritual growth and that I truly had a servant's heart to care and be there for everyone around me. Everyone suddenly burst into applause. I've always disliked getting that kind of attention, but I tried to be respectful about it and quickly thanked them.

Colossians 3:17 says something I was truly trying to live out, even though I didn't know it in my head yet. The first half of the verse says, *"Whatever you do in word or deed, **do** all in the name of the Lord Jesus"* (NASB, emphasis mine). All I wanted was to serve as God called me to serve. If He called me to do something, I'd go do it, no questions asked. At the time, there was nothing greater than Him and what He would call me to do.

Chapter 8

Let's Be Real

I didn't quite understand the sin in my life yet. I had done a few bad things in my life, but I didn't view them as sin should be viewed—as something that produces death. I only saw them as bad things to avoid, nothing more and nothing less. I acknowledged some of my sins, but never had true remorse or sorrow over them. Sometimes, I asked God to break my heart for what breaks His, but I can't remember ever having heartbreaking remorse over my sins. Not understanding everything, I still renounced and repented of them because I understood that it was the right thing to do. The easiest and most common thing I asked God for in regard to my sins, was to renew my mind and replace my sinful lifestyle with a life lived in the Spirit of God.

I didn't care about getting saved for the sole purpose of going to heaven like most Christians I know. If I happened to die and go to heaven, it would be a bonus to the relationship I have with God. I simply wanted to give Jesus Christ my all; I wanted to give Him my life—every ounce of my being. When I told Him that, He placed it on my heart to love those younger than me like an older brother should love his younger siblings. When I felt this being placed on my heart, I felt that I was doing this as a sibling in Christ. If I had the ability, I would want to prevent every one of them from having to feel the pain I had gone through. Since I never felt like anyone cared about me growing up, I made it a goal to make sure that those younger than me knew that at least two people cared about them. I wanted them to know that I care, and far more importantly, that God cares. My heart broke for them far more than it did for my own life.

I searched for a Bible verse that encompassed everything I was feeling that summer, and I finally found one during one of our student church services a few weeks after my last summer trip. It's John 15:13, which says, *"Greater love has no one than this, that one lay down his life for his friends"* (NASB). I think that this refers not only to laying down your life physically, but also spiritually and emotionally. It's not only talking about taking a bullet for a friend, like most people think of it in the physical sense, but it means that we are to connect with them as well. It means connecting with what's going on in their life, both spiritually and emotionally by putting ourselves aside and doing what we can to intentionally help them grow.

At one of our church services, John 15:13 was mentioned along with a story in the Old Testament about a time when King David was hiding in a cave with his most honorable and trustworthy men. All he wanted was a cup of water from the well where he had drunk water when he was younger. Unfortunately, the well was in enemy-controlled territory with armed camps all around. Yet, David's honorable and trustworthy men went to that well, fighting through the multitude of enemies for a simple cup of water (2 Samuel 23:13–17).

This act of service may not seem significant to you, but it was one of the most heartfelt moments I've ever experienced. They were willing to sacrifice who they were for someone they cared about and loved. I started to feel that deep in my heart. Even though I had never experienced anyone making that type of sacrifice for me, I wanted to give that kind of care to others. I wanted to sacrifice all that I could for the ones I loved even if they didn't feel the same way toward me. At that time, the students at church were the main group of people that I felt God was calling me to care about.

Later that weekend, I had a strange moment. It was a mixture of a déjà vu moment and a flashback in the form of a dream. Yeah, it was very odd. This is when I first became fully aware of God's miraculous hand in my birth. Simply put, I had an out-of-body experience. I remember having a bird's-eye view of my room with myself as a newborn in a hospital bed, surrounded by my parents and their friends and family. At the same time, I envisioned God hugging tightly to His newborn baby boy, whispering in his ear, "I love you. I care about you. It doesn't matter what the rest of the world says. I will always be here for you. I will always love you."

This was the first time in my life that I truly felt like someone cared about me and loved me. I knew that caring heart and love was all from God. I haven't had a doubt from that moment on that He loves me; He always will, and I wanted to live my life in the same way for others. His love is the same for you no matter what you've been through. He loves you, and He always will. It's my hope and prayer that there's no truth more real than that one in your life.

Chapter 9

The Unqualified Calling

After experiencing God's love, my life didn't instantly become perfect. Life was still difficult for me after that summer. I still had feelings of wanting to die, but my desire to help others was one of the few reasons I gave myself for continuing. I cared about the younger students more than myself. Since God still had me around, I decided I wanted to do things for Christ, even though there was still this pain in my heart. The negative, suicidal thoughts of wanting to die have been some of the greatest sins I struggled against. These thoughts would enter my mind, but to survive I had to give my life to God and trust Him in every moment. When I cave in to these thoughts, I need to confess them as sin, like any other sin I commit. I must remind myself daily that God cares about us and loves us more than anything else. Whatever negative thoughts we may have need to be overtaken with the truth that He loves us and cares for us. Our thoughts should be consumed with the goodness of God, not the destructiveness of anything sinful. Even if something doesn't seem destructive, if it's not about God or for Him, it will destroy us.

God isn't some quick-fix solution or a genie in a lamp to whom we make a wish or prayer and He does what we ask. If He were like that, then He would be something to us, not someone. This Christian life is all about having a relationship with Him. A relationship isn't meeting someone, getting them to do what we want, then never talking with them again. Every relationship, including the one we have with God, is a continual process. Some relationships need other people to step in and keep you there, and that's what I needed in the beginning of my personal relationship with God during my senior year in high school. That year, I had two people who were a constant encouragement. One of them was a freshman, and the other was a senior like I was. They both cared about me relentlessly, with what I could only describe as the love of Christ.

I believe I would've attempted suicide again if they had not come into my life. I had God, of course, but as humans, we also need a connection with other people. It felt like I had no other people in my life who genuinely cared besides them, so if they hadn't been there, I doubt if anyone else would've cared. Every day, my senior friend would give me the biggest hug and intentionally ask how I was doing. You know how everyone starts a conversation with, "How are you?" as the greeting, but they don't care to know how we are? Most days when I saw my friend, I felt like she truly cared when she asked me how I was. From the time I got to know her in our senior year, I saw her as someone who intentionally cares. It felt like she always went above and beyond in expressing God's love for me.

What if someone you know, friend or not, came and asked you this: "If I died or took my own life, would you care?" The natural answer should be yes, Christian or not. But it's not natural for us to be ready for the why question right behind it: "Why would you care?" Saying, "just because" or "it's the right thing to do" didn't suffice for me, but that's what I got from most people. It may be the right thing to do, but people who are struggling need to hear the details of why they matter to you. They need to hear an answer that shows that you care about them. What would you say if someone asked, "What specific parts of me and my individuality would you miss if I were gone?" The individual's qualities need to be spoken and heard. This happened when I opened up to both my friends, making them aware of the pain concealed in my heart. After that, they expressed what my life meant to them, and how their lives would be affected if I killed myself. No one else had cared that much. I was truly blessed to have them in my life at that time.

I know that God views each of us as precious in His eyes, but when I see Jesus face-to-face in heaven, I would want to know the specific "why" behind His care for me. It meant a lot when these two friends said the specifics of why I was precious in their eyes; it'll mean so much more when the One who has always cared for me, even when it felt like everyone else in the world was against me, speaks His mind on why I matter to Him.

I always thought that if anything happened to me, everyone would carry on with their lives like nothing happened, but these friends helped change my perspective on that. There will always be a few people who truly do care. There's a massive difference between someone saying something simple like, "I would care" and someone else going into the deep details of why they care. When someone expresses deep details of why they don't want you to die with a choked-up voice and tears in their eyes, their genuine concern is obvious to see. Let's be people who have genuine concern for others and care about them. We can't do that well if we don't know them, so we need to let ourselves be close to others. At the end of every day, we should care about others more than we did at the beginning of our day.

I started serving in student ministry during my senior year in high school, and I have continued to serve till this day. The average student ministry leader I grew up around was full of energy and energetic all the time for the students, but that was never me. I know my personality didn't come anywhere close to the typical student ministry leader, but I truly believe that God has called me into this ministry.

Over the years, I've been questioned and ridiculed by students, parents, other leaders, and even pastors. I may be one of the most unqualified people for my ministry role if I were judged solely on my personality. On the contrary, I believe that when it comes to ministry, God doesn't ask us to qualify for the job before He calls us into the work. It's the exact opposite. He calls us first, and then He qualifies us. He always qualifies the called; He doesn't always call those who seem qualified. If you desire and strive to live for Him above all else, He'll call you into something, and then that calling will become your qualification. If He can use me in student ministry, He can use you wherever He's calling you to serve.

Consider one example of how I was following Christ as a high school senior. At the time, we weren't a worshipful student ministry. There would be many weeks when no one even stood up unless the leader asked everyone to, because they weren't "feeling it." I decided to live out the simple idea of "If I said I'm going to live for You, Christ, I'm actually going to do it." After that, there were weeks when I decided to stand up during worship even though I was the only one out of a crowd of around 100 students. As weeks passed, other students started standing, and over time, their hearts started to change into more worshipful hearts toward God. Today, some of those students are worship leaders.

It doesn't feel like I did anything big, but I had a tiny part in helping make the student ministry a more worshipful environment. It wasn't my intention, but God used me to help make it happen. I simply wanted to worship my Lord, Savior, and Creator because I love Him. I didn't care what other people thought, and above all else I had a desire to live for Christ no matter what. If you're a student in a youth ministry, become that catalyst. Become the change that you see needs to happen. Even if you don't see a need for change but you believe what God says is true, then stand up for Him and live for Him. Have a heart solely focused and desiring to live for Christ above all else. Don't worry about the other people around you. Live for Him. At the end of the Gospel, when Peter questioned

Jesus about John, He responded, *"What is that to you? You must follow me"* (John 21:22). We mustn't be concerned with turning to the left or right but stay committed to the path of following Christ. Read Proverbs 4:25–27. We must have complete, undivided focus and attention on Him.

If you're not a student, but you're older, I'm asking you to pray for the students. I really mean it! Pray, pray, pray, and pray some more! These students are vital to the world we live in and for the future. It feels like there are few Christian adults who have a fire to live for Jesus, so it would be terrible if these students grow up and repeat this lifestyle we're living out.

God, I pray You give them a heart for You above all else. Let them fall deeply in love with You and strive to live for You in every waking moment of their life. I also want to pray for older men and women to mentor these students to follow You. I ask this not only for our city, but for the rest of the nation and the rest of the world. Amen.

Worship is such a powerful thing that God uses to connect us to Him. Right now, I'm deeply praying for at least one of the students in my church's student ministry to become a catalyst like I was 12 years ago at my old church.

God light a fire in these students' hearts to worship You with all that they are! Let the life that they live be all about You! I pray that You're the greatest desire in their lives, in every step they take, and every word they speak! In the name of Jesus Christ. Amen.

Some of the words in the worship songs we sing can be spoken out as prayers. The line of a song I'm starting to listen to right now is, "My life is Yours; my hope is in You only." Immediately, this prayer came to mind:

God, I've given my life to You. Everything about me is for You. Help me to live and continue to live for You in all circumstances. I desire to live for You above all else. When life gets hard, and I want to give up, I know that You're my only hope. I ask You to be a consistent reminder that You're my only hope. Nothing else will give me hope, and if it appears like it will, it will only be temporary. I know that the hope You give me will last forever and ever, for all eternity. I don't only pray this for myself, but for my students and everyone else around me. Amen.

A single line in the song inspired my prayer, so imagine what your conversations with God will be like with all the other biblical truths in the rest of the song and every other song that expresses biblical truths. These songs are deeply connected with God's Word. Scripture is alive throughout so much worship music. Romans 12:1–2 is a great example about giving our life to Him. Also, Psalms 39:7, 62:5, and 33:20–22 talk about how our hope is only in Him. There are so many truths in God's Word right in line with the worship songs that we sing. One of my favorite songs, which has parts taken from Scripture, is "Better Is One Day," based on Psalm 84:10. The only way we can become familiar with the connection between His Word and these songs is when we get to know Him and His Word.

Over the years, I've had some students who felt completely unlovable and hopeless; they thought that no one would ever care about them at all. I've said some crazy things back to their comments. For example, I've frequently said, "I care about you far more than myself." It's not because I must do so as a leader, but because I truly do care, and that's one way that I show how I care. No matter who it is, most of the time, people will focus on themselves before they look toward others, if they even go that far. I don't want to have any part in that kind of life. If God will allow it, I want to love in the exact same way that He loves.

At times, I've also asked God to bring new pain into my life, so I can go through the same hard times as my students. I asked God this so I could relate with my students a lot easier and help bring them closer to Christ through the hard times they're facing. Most of the times when I asked Him, He did it. After all, my intention in asking was for His glory to be shown, and in the end, the situation ended up glorifying Him and bringing the students closer to Him.

One of my crazier ones is like something that Paul said in Romans 9:3, but I didn't know the verse at the time. I said, "If God would allow it, I would gladly give up my own salvation for your sake, so you could know Christ." Here's what Paul said in Romans 9:3, *"For I could wish that I myself were cursed and cut off from Christ for the sake of my people."* On the surface, that would be a ridiculous statement for one of us to say since we would be sacrificing our own relationship with Christ for someone else to have a relationship with Christ. That's one request that God most likely wouldn't ever do because Jesus is the only one worthy enough to do something like that, but it shows my heart of what I would be willing to give for someone else to have that deep intimate relationship of knowing Christ.

These things may sound beyond crazy to you, but I truly do care about the students God has placed in my life. It's all because of Christ. I want to live for Him above all else, and His love for me turned into love for others. He's where it's all coming out from. As I've lived these past years serving in student ministry and moving toward the future, Jesus Christ continues to be the most important part of my life. He and His Word will constantly be cherished in my heart. Unfortunately, the part I've recently failed at is even though I constantly feel this in my heart, I don't always express it with my words as I should. When that happens, what I feel in my heart has lost its worth since it's meant for someone else other than me, so we must live out our faith through both our words and actions.

Chapter 10

What's the Point? Is It Even Worth It?

If you're feeling anything like I did when I fought against my negative and suicidal thoughts, you may feel like you're in the middle of a valley. You see the walls of the valley all around, but there's no escape. It's overwhelming, making you feel so powerless that you don't know what to do. You can quit and give up right there or keep walking in the dark depths of the valley hoping to find the exit one day. We all go through valleys in our lives. We all face hard times. As long as I'm on earth walking my path, the walls of my valley will get higher or lower depending on the day, but the day I'll finally leave the valley is the day I'll meet my Maker in heaven.

I believe this idea of the valley is the same for all of us. We were born down here in the valley, because this is a sinful world that we were born into and live in. As we're walking through the deep darkness of this valley, we need to keep our eyes focused on the sky, constantly looking up to God. He'll shine His light onto our dark path. He is our hope. He is our rescue from the depths of sin and shame. The day we see His face is when we'll leave the valley, but as of now, we're still in the valley, and we need to have all our focus and attention on Him. If we don't look to Him, we'll easily get lost and make our journey through the valley so much harder than it needs to be. Even though we could be lost for years, no matter how lost we are, we can easily turn to Christ in a moment and follow Him.

After sharing my story, I feel like it's extremely important to address a certain topic before anything else. It's a sensitive topic for a lot of people, but there's also a desperate need to discuss it. It's suicide. It would be completely truthful of me to write the words, "I don't feel like anyone cares about me or loves me," in many parts of my story. That phrase was something I constantly felt while growing up. This constant pain in my life made me believe things that I'd tell myself like, "You're a waste of space. You're worthless. It would've been better if you were never born. Don't think that anyone loves you. No one even cares about you. If you'd die, no one would even come to your funeral. You're always going to be alone. What's the point of going on? Is it even worth it?" I kept these thoughts to myself; I didn't dare share with anyone else. That's how my heart felt, but not writing it or speaking it doesn't make it any less true. Keeping it in like I did doesn't make you feel better.

Maybe you think of yourself this way, or maybe you know someone else who does. It's also possible that someone you know is viewing themselves this way even though you don't know that they are. Suicide is something so dirty that no one wants to touch it, and people try to avoid talking about it at all costs. I can't remember the last time someone talked about it at church. Unfortunately, it's something that gets brushed under the rug far too often. It feels so wrong to say that, but that's the current reality for most people. As Christians, we should be helping those who are weak and hurting no matter the magnitude of their hurt. We don't need to have the answers to the problem, but we should simply show that we care.

People who have thoughts of suicide have an internal struggle with opening up and sharing. They almost never feel like it's safe to share what's going on, so they usually keep their thoughts inside and feel like the best thing they can do is to keep silent and live with their pain. Sadly, some people hurt to the point that they give up, and we just push them to the side like they're nothing. That's what our actions are expressing even if that isn't our intention. As Christians, we should care so much that people who are hurting have a safe and secure place they can go when they're in pain. That place should be us, as the church, since God has called us to love and take care of those who are hurting.

Sometimes, hurting people come out into the open with their struggles, and everyone desperately tries to show that they care because it seems like what they're sharing "comes out of nowhere." The truth is that the pain and suicidal thoughts have been there for a while, but too often, we are so focused on ourselves that we're blind to what's happening with people around us. In fact, we may have unintentionally given the impression that we don't care about anyone else. To the person who's uneasy about sharing their struggles, having everyone try to do something good for them can be overwhelming, and it may close them off from everyone once again. It becomes a complicated situation, which can easily trap them within their feelings.

The question we have to ask ourselves is "Where were we before the hurting person opened up? What are we doing to prevent people we know from experiencing such loneliness and isolation, instead of only trying to fix the problem? If we really want to fix it, then we need to try to prevent it before it becomes such a critical issue. I truly believe that prevention is the best way to fix most of life's issues. How do we prevent suicide? The answer is to simply care about people who are hurting. I know it's a ridiculously simple solution, but most people who struggle with suicidal thoughts don't feel loved or cared for. I remember two people in my life who cared about me, and I was able to see God's love through them. Every time we interact with someone, we have an opportunity to show kindness and show that we care about them. We need to take advantage of this opportunity, and through our actions, the hurting people among us may see the love of Christ.

For a person who's having suicidal thoughts, who do you think is the most dangerous person to them? Is it the people being mean to them? That's the expected answer, but I disagree. Is it them? Maybe they are their own worst enemy. Even though it's true that people can invite their own sufferings, especially in suicide-related situations, but I disagree with that answer. I'd say the most dangerous people are the ones within arm's reach who could help but refuse to be a helping hand. They see the person's pain but tell themselves that they're not going to be a part of that. They reject being there for the one in need. We can also apply this in a spiritual sense; that is, as Christians, we know that everyone needs Christ. How many of us Christians see someone else who doesn't know Christ, but we're not even willing to share Christ with them? We refuse to help the one in need. We need to go and help those in need.

There are people around us who face thoughts of suicide every day. Many of them are the last people we'd suspect of having such struggles. I know because I've been one of these people. So many times, I didn't want to continue to the next day, but whether we like it or not, the next day is coming. We can easily make the choice to no longer be there that next day; that choice would remove us from the lives of everyone who would be left. That would be one of the worst things we could do to someone who cares about us. We may feel like we aren't needed, but God wants to use our lives to impact everyone around us. He has us alive for a reason, and that reason is to glorify Him. When we glorify Him, we are what everyone around us needs in order to see Him.

The city I live in is one of the wealthier cities in the country, but our rate of suicide and depression is also one of the highest in the country. Life is hard. No one can deny that. The solution isn't in getting more material stuff, because no matter how people try to fill their emptiness with things, they will still feel empty. Jesus Christ is the only one who can remove the emptiness in our hearts.

What do we do when life feels too hard, and we want to quit

at life? You don't quit. I know it's not an easy solution. Believe me, giving up is the last thing you want to do because it will be the last thing you do, and you wouldn't be able to make any more choices after that. Having people in your life who encourage and support you to continue to live for Christ is what's deeply needed. This has been a hard area for me to live out. If I'm being completely honest, I'd say I don't encourage and support others enough even though I'm part of a great church with a great community of believers.

I don't have all the answers, but I'm trying to live out His Word, which He has placed in my heart. I feel like I have more days of struggle than days of success. When I'm living in this sin, at the end of my day, I come face-to-face with all my pain, and I feel so worthless every time. It doesn't matter whether I finished hanging out with church friends only five minutes ago, the hurts keep resurfacing in my heart. For me, the hurts come flooding in strongest when I come to a stop at the end of my day; even though my work for the day is done, my mind is still racing at a hundred miles per hour. As I lie down some nights, the pain is so real and crushing that it is hard to breathe. It feels like no one cares, and it makes me want to stop breathing as well. My nights usually end with a heavy heart, sorrow, and feelings of loneliness; there are a few nights with tears. If that doesn't give a vivid description of the reality of sin producing death in our hearts, I don't know what does.

There isn't only this physical form of suicide, but there is also a spiritual side of it that people face every day. Each time we sin, it's as if we're trying to commit suicide to our soul. It's unintentional, but it's the reality of what we do in sin. Suicide comes from an individual not wanting to live anymore, and the only result that sin produces is death (James 1:15). The opposite of death is life, and there is only life in Jesus Christ. We must constantly be desiring to focus on Him rather than any sinful or ungodly things.

If you are struggling with suicidal thoughts, these are heavy things to hear, but I encourage you to keep on fighting the good fight, persevere, and stay continually focused on Christ. This is advice I try to live out, and I encourage you to do the same. If you're not part of a good church, first and foremost, I encourage you to find a good Bible-teaching church—both in terms of what they preach and how they do everything. Fighting the good fight is harder without people in your life. I've lived most of my life without community, but I don't recommend that. It's hard to do life alone. In fact, it's near impossible. If you're involved in a good Bible-based church, I encourage you to find people there who will encourage you and live step by step with you in your walk with Christ. Above all else, know that the love of Christ is never-ending and all-powerful. No matter what your life has been like, He views you as His child and loves you as such.

In 1 John 3:1, the Bible says *"See what great love the Father has lavished on us, that we should be called children of God! And that is what we are!"* You are God's child, and He loves you deeply beyond what any words can express. He loves you so much! Turn to Him and let yourself be loved! If you're already a Christian and living for Him, help others see Jesus and help Jesus love them by loving them yourself. We love because He first loved us. God initiated everything good in our lives, and if we're living for Christ, we will naturally want to give all those good things to those around us— especially one of the best things He has for us, His love. If God's love is equivalent to all the sand on the beaches and in the ocean, then the hurt and pain we feel don't even match up to a single grain of sand. It can't even compare. All the pain is a waste of space in the face of God and His love for us. There's nothing more important than Him.

I know so many Christians who have the mindset that while they're alive they will try to gain as much as they can; then once they die, that's when they'll be with Christ. That's the wrong mindset; it should be the opposite. While we're alive, our life should be all about Christ, but when we die, it's all about gaining everything, which, ironically, also happens to be Christ, since He is the greatest thing we could ever gain (Philippians 1:20–21). In the last part of this passage in Philippians, Paul mentions that his life is about Christ, but when he dies, that's when he'll gain everything. Paul says that no matter what happens to him, through this life or through his death, every bit of who he is, it's all for Christ. His life is all for Christ, but what about ours? If you truly know Christ and live for Him, then everything else becomes insignificant in comparison to Him. Jesus Christ becomes your reason for living. He is all we need. It seems like so many people don't value Him as that important. What's the point of our life? Jesus Christ is, or He should be. Is He worth living out this life? He absolutely is. Get to know Him. When I say get to know Him, I mean have a personal, intimate relationship with Him; then, you will see that He is worth it. Now, can each of us say that He's worth it in our own story?

Chapter 11

How Do I Share My Story?

Every Christian has a story that needs to be shared. This is the best way we can see how we're connected to God, and it's the best tool in our arsenal for letting others know about Jesus Christ because it's a personal relationship that can't be denied. We need to know how to share our story. It can be a challenge since no one story is identical to another. They're all unique; some are similar, but never the same. However, every believer's story talks about the presence of sin and the presence of Jesus Christ; the rest of the details are unique to that individual. In all the stories I've heard, there are three main areas: (1) what the individual's life was like before knowing Christ, (2) how/ when they met Christ, and (3) what their life is like after meeting Christ.

When it comes to our life before Christ, sin was a constant presence in our life. This part of my story includes the times when I tried to end my life and felt all alone as a result of how everyone treated me. I may look like the victim, but every time someone hurt me, God gave me an opportunity to forgive them. By not forgiving them, I committed a wrong against God. I sinned against Him in those moments. I can't blame those people for my choice of refusing to forgive them. Yeah, they probably also sinned when they hurt me, but I also sinned when I refused to forgive them when I had the chance. They made their choice, and I made mine no matter how big or small it may seem. Every moment brings an opportunity to make a significant choice because every choice can easily turn into sin. Just as easy as it is to make that choice of falling into sin, we can easily be turned around into the loving arms of Christ, all by His grace and forgiveness. God gives us opportunities to turn to Him. If we're following Him in those moments, we can also live out His grace and forgiveness for others. The opportunities are always there, and I truly hope that everyone who hurt me took advantage of the opportunities Christ most likely presented to them later in their life. I hope that they know Christ and have a relationship with Him today.

Some sins are more obvious than others. The culture in which we live affects how we view sin. I grew up knowing I wasn't perfect, but I didn't really understand my sin. I was a nice kid, doing good and nice things for others, but it wasn't enough. It wasn't about doing enough good to not be considered bad. Sin isn't just bad things; it goes much deeper than that. Sin is so bad that it separates us from God. It separates us from the One who gives and breathes out life; this separation ultimately causes death in our lives. What specific thing separates us from God? Why does it, or why would it separate us from God? What's so bad about us being separated from Him? Why should I care that I'm separated from Him? What if I can't recognize what's separating me from Him? These are good questions to ask when we're thinking about our life before we came to Christ.

I can't tell you exactly what to say when you're thinking about this part of your story, but usually it's full of hurt and pain. You know your own life far better than I do. I wish I could tell you exactly what to say, but we would have to know the deepest parts of each other's hearts. The best advice I can give you is to look at the hurts, pains, and sufferings you have faced. Those are the things that are usually in everyone's story before they meet Christ. Since they're in just about everyone's story, they will draw the attention of people who have faced some of those same things. That's the best way to start sharing your story. It's also good to look for things that distance you from God, especially if you haven't faced any hard times. None of us are perfect, but we all have done things that have separated us from Him.

The second part of our story is when we meet Christ. In my story, I'm not sure when the exact moment was, but I do know it happened over the summer before my senior year in high school. So, I believe my salvation in Christ wasn't a single moment, but a process. I believe it's the same way with many people; it's a process of coming from living in sin to living in Christ. I first saw the change happening in my life during that summer, but it very well could have started years before. You could be in the beginning process now, or it's possible that you're just starting to see what God is doing in your heart.

In this part of everyone's story, there's a mixture of both the presence of sin and the presence of Jesus Christ. It's a massive transition from the very worst thing to the very best thing. It's a change-of-the-heart moment. It's extremely rare that this moment is a pretty moment. It usually starts ugly and gets a little nicer, but there's still some ugliness in there. It looks ugly because of the presence of sin and being real and open about the sin deep in your heart. Being real with anyone is almost never a pretty moment, especially being real with God about our sin for the first time. We're going from the worst of the worst to the best of the best. In a person's life, this may be the hardest thing they do because of how exponentially massive the change is, and it usually happens in such a small amount of time.

"It's crazy. It's insane. It's impossible. It's life-changing. It's the best thing that happened to me. It's overwhelmingly joyous." Those are a few things I've heard people say about this moment. Jesus Christ is really the difference maker that makes it all possible. Who is He? What did He do for you? When did you meet Him? How did you find out about Him? Did anyone tell you about Him? How did you feel

He spoke to you, and how did you feel when He did? These are good questions to ask when we recall the moment that we met Him.

This moment always consists of God's love. It comes in many different forms and fashions. I've seen people experience His love mainly through His Word and other people. In my own story, I felt His love through my own thoughts and other people. My thoughts were from the Bible, but I didn't know it then. At the time, they just gave me comfort. The negative experiences I had before meeting Christ were there to contrast with the positive experience of His love. This amplified His love so much more and made it that much more powerful.

John 15:13 says, *"Greater love has no one than this: to lay down one's life for one's friends."* This is the greatest love—to lay down your life for others. That's exactly what Jesus did for us. He didn't just take a bullet for us or hang on the cross in our place. While He was hanging on that cross, waiting for His death, He took all the punishment we deserved because of our sin. Not just the sin of one or two people, but all humanity, from Adam and Eve, to right now, to who knows when the last person will ever live. He took the punishment for all our sin in that single moment on the cross. Now, that's true love. That's overwhelming love. His love has no boundaries whatsoever. That's greater than we could even imagine. Some people view God's love as deep as an ocean, but the ocean has its limit on how deep it can go. God's love doesn't, so it's more like the stars and heavens. The cosmos is so vast, and so much of it is unexplored. I believe outer space is there to show the greatness of God and how big He is. I can imagine Him in heaven looking forward to us discovering the next big thing in space, just so He can share more and more, again and again, for all eternity. God and His love have no limits or boundaries, and His love is directed at all of us. All we need to do is accept it as it is.

Now comes the part of our story that happens after we meet

Christ. When we met Christ, we saw His love for us, accepted it, and let Him overtake the sin living in our hearts, so what's next? In my story, this part is where I'm involved in the church and serving in our student ministry, which I'm continuing to do today even though God sent me to a different church in 2011. We need to know Him well enough to hear when He calls us into something. God has called me to serve in student ministry, but it may be something completely different for you.

Most of the time, what happens after salvation consists of growing closer to Christ and helping to bring others closer to Him. The best way this growth happens is within the church. Some of my favorite weekends at church are the ones when we do baptisms. At my church, each person who is baptized has their testimony read, which is why these are some of my favorite weekends. Hearing the stories of God redeeming people from their sin tugs at my heartstrings. From little ones in our kids' ministry all the way to those who are in their 70s, these are beautiful moments. In case you don't know what baptism is, let me explain briefly. Baptism is something we Christians do to symbolize that the sin in our life has been buried (being submerged under the water) and that we have been raised to life in Christ (being brought up out of the water). When someone is baptized, they are not saved in that moment; rather, they are professing in front of their family in Christ that they have already been saved, and are, therefore, committing to live their life for Christ.

I suggest you find a good church that's true in both what is spoken and how it's done. What is being taught? Is it accurate with God's Word? In Acts 17:11, it mentions a group of people listening to Paul. Every day they heard from him, they checked for themselves that everything spoken matched up with who God is and what He's about by looking at His Word. Since God is the One who spoke out His Word, we know it's trustworthy and the best guide for what He wants for us. How is church being done? Is it matching up with God's heart for how He wants church to be done? Is it centered on Jesus Christ? Is it about bringing people closer to Him? Is the church giving to the poor, powerless, and those with needs? Not just locally, but around the world as well. Is discipleship happening at that church with older men investing in the lives of younger men? Are older women investing in the lives of younger women? Are older couples investing in the lives of younger couples? Can the rich and poor come together? Can people of different ethnicities come together? Does the church have groups in which old and young and rich and poor can come together? Can these groups come together and study God's Word, share life's burdens, support one another, and assist one another when the need arises? Can these groups simply enjoy one another's company?

Does the church have a big church mindset? I say that keeping in mind that the church isn't buildings, but it's people. Everyone who believes that Jesus Christ is their Lord and Savior is part of this big church. Do they have this mindset by praying for other local churches? Do they not envy what other churches are doing when things are going well for them, but are supportive in what God has called them to do? Do they encourage other churches when things aren't going well for them? Although there is no perfect church, look for one that's striving for these things. Look for the heart of Jesus Christ, when you're looking for a church. Church is a truly beautiful thing. When church is done in the way that God desires us to live it out, it's like a second family, or even a first family for some people.

It's true that there are times that I've seen church when it was not so beautiful. In a recent student ministry service at our church, the main idea was this: the church should be your haven. Growing up in church before I started serving, it never felt like it was a haven for me. Most weeks, it was the opposite. I hated being around the people there. When I gave my life to Christ, I didn't care anymore whether it was a haven for me, but I wanted it to be one for the other students around me. If you're a student, help make your youth group a haven for the other students around you. Church should be a place where everyone feels comfortable. Having church be a haven shouldn't be our end goal; living for Christ and having a life that represents Him in every moment should be our primary goal. Live for Him. You may be the deciding factor in how those around you view Christ, but your focus should be on living for Christ more than being that deciding factor. That's where the real difference happens.

What does your life look like after you have met Jesus Christ? What's different? Is anything similar? Is He calling you into anything? How is your story connected to His story? This part of the story isn't only about what has happened since we met Christ, but it is also the life we're going to live from now on. What's next? What does our future look like? How is God going to grow me? What role do we now have to play in the church? Can He grow others through me? Can He grow me through growing others? These are questions we can ask ourselves when we're thinking about our life after we've met Christ; they are all about moving forward. When we're living for Christ, we're constantly moving forward. Sometimes, it may not look like it because change is a slow process. We need to trust God in those moments. Trusting God is the most important thing we can always do, good or bad.

Let's take one last look at how our story compares to God's story. Let's view it like a book. In a book, there are chapters, pages, paragraphs, sentences, words, letters, and punctuation. If our story is only a part of God's big story, then what do you think your story is in the book of God's story? I view my story as a single stroke of the pen of a single letter in God's big story. It's so tiny in comparison to God's grand story. I consider it a privilege to even be invited into His story. You can be the judge of your own story, but if you're viewing God as He is, I don't think you'll see it much different from the way

I view my story. Our stories can be part of God's story, but in the grand sweep of history, they would only be a very tiny part of His story. Yet, He loves us and cares about us deeper than anyone else ever could.

Whatever happens in your story, Jesus Christ should be the central attraction and greatness of it all. In my story, people are attracted to my miracle birth and my struggle with suicidal thoughts. After all, these are the main parts of my story. People are attracted to the miracle because they are encouraged that something good like that happened. Others are attracted to the discussion of issues related to suicide because they've had similar feelings and can relate on a deeper level, or they may know someone else who struggles in that way. Those two events in my life may have an emotional connection with your heart; however, they are not the central greatness of my story. Jesus Christ is. These experiences are incomparably insignificant in comparison to Jesus Christ and what He's done in my life. He is truly the amazing One. No matter how the other parts of my story attract your heart, Jesus Christ should attract your heart above everything else. It is the same with your story; no matter what circumstances attract someone's heart, Jesus Christ should attract their heart far more than anything else.

He should be our greatest desire and the center of our life. Within the church culture that I've been raised in, I've noticed that the married life has been idolized. My guess is that everyone thinks that the married couple has it all together, but it's very possible they don't. We can all have a nice outer appearance, but there's usually something going on in the heart of each one of us, married or not. Unfortunately, the opinion of those who are married seems to be valued far more than that of someone who is single, separated, divorced, or widowed. I'm saying this as someone who's been single for 29 years and counting and has been very involved in the church for the past 12 years. Our value shouldn't be defined by our marital status. Our value should be based on Christ alone. No matter your marital status, let your life be all about Christ. If you're single for five years, live for Christ in everything. If you're single for 30 or more years, live for Christ in everything. If you're married, both of you should live for Christ in everything. If you were married and now separated, live for Christ in everything. If you're divorced, live for Christ in everything. If you're a widow, live for Christ in everything. Let your life be all about Christ, no matter what. Nothing else compares to Him, and everything else is insignificant to Him, so live a life that is all about Him, always. We need to stop valuing people based on the circumstances of their life and start valuing them as a brother or sister in Christ, or even a potential brother or sister in Christ.

Chapter 12

The Attractive Miracle

Every testimony has miracles in it. A miracle is a supernatural work of God. Looking back at my testimony, what would you guess the miracles in it were? Most people would say that the only miracle is what happened at my birth. I wasn't supposed to be alive, but by God's power, I lived. That's a powerful miracle, but not the greatest and most attractive one.

When I say attractive, I'm not referring to a romantic type of attraction, but in the sense that something draws our attention. With that said, what would you view as the most attractive part of my story? To me, it's God's constant love in the midst of my hurt and pain. No matter how much pain I was in or how alone I was, God was always there caring for me and loving me. It didn't matter whether it was pain I caused myself by my own sin or pain others directed at me, God still cared about and loved me. One of the main ways I saw God connect my story to His story was by the pain I went through.

Just as our story is the best tool we can use to share Christ with others, the pain in our story is the best tool God uses to bring us closer to Him. It may bring us close to Him, but I believe it's wrong to ask for hurts and pains to be brought into our life. There was a time that I did that for the sake of my students, but I now believe it was wrong of me to do that. That's not something that can truly be justified. It did end up glorifying God by bringing them closer to

Him because God can use the negative choices and sufferings we face to glorify Himself.

Even though I lived with the constant pain of my own negative, self-inflicting thoughts of suicide, I'm aware that God's love for me as His child has been even more constant. God was always there caring for and loving me. In the middle of these sinful thoughts, He cared about me and freed me of my sin. Even when I go back to my sin, He still cares about me and is willing to cleanse the sin from my life each time I go back to Him, confessing my sins. That's His love. That's the greatest miracle God could do, and it's the most attractive miracle He can produce.

Everything I've said about how God loves me and cares about me also applies to you. He also loves you and cares about you. No matter what you've gone through, know that He also views you as His child, and He loves you far more than you could possibly imagine.

In Luke 6:45, the Bible says: *"A good man brings good things out of the good stored up in his heart, and an evil man brings evil things out of the evil stored up in his heart. For the mouth speaks what the heart is full of."*

Everything we say and do comes from the deepest desires of our hearts. The greatest things we value begin at the heart. My heart hasn't always been about Christ, but it now desires to be about Him more than anything else.

Has God produced an attractive miracle in your life? Has it reached to your heart? What's your heart all about? If you don't know and want a clue, look at what you say and do. Our words and actions always reflect what's going on in our hearts (Luke 6:45). Do you like what you see, or would you like some change to happen?

Only God can create that change. We have to recognize our sin, be broken by it, renounce and repent of our sin, turn away from it, start to let God renew our mind and heart with a mind and heart that matches with His, and replace our life of sin with a life of living for Christ. These things are true for the person dealing with sin, whether they claim to be a Christian who is following Christ or not. The only way we can do these things is by God's power alone. We can't create a miracle; only God can.

Conclusion

Earlier, I asked how we are connected to God. We walked through the different parts of a story; we looked at the parts in our story and in God's story. We saw how both stories were connected and realized what our story should look like. Then I shared my story, along with some thoughts on suicide. We saw how to share our own story, and lastly, we looked at the most important part in everyone's story.

With everything that we've looked at, what connects us to God? The connection isn't a what, but who—Jesus Christ. He is the connection between us and God. Without Him, it's impossible for us to have connection to God. I know some people believe that they have that connection with God just because they feel connected to something spiritual. Don't be deceived; God isn't the only spiritual being out there. There are countless other ones as well, and none of them are good. The Triune God (the Father, Son, and Holy Spirit) is the only good one. We swim in extremely dangerous waters when we're connected to one who is not Christ. Know that if we want to be connected to God, we must know Jesus Christ first. If we aren't connected to Christ, then we'll never be connected to God.

Jesus Christ went to great lengths to demonstrate his love for us by leaving perfection in heaven and coming to a messed-up world, by living the perfect life without sin and dying on the cross to take the place of all our sin, and being raised up from the grave three days later. Jesus Christ has always desired to connect His life with ours. No matter how dirty or filthy our lives may be, He wants to wash all the filth away; we can't say we're too messed up to be connected with Him. However, we can all say that we're not good enough, and that would be completely true. None of us are good enough, but He still loves us beyond comprehension and wants to connect His life with ours. His love for us should always be the catalyst when we give our life to Christ. It's what connects us with Him.

As I finish writing, my biggest hope for you is that you've come closer to Christ in some way as you read my story. If you didn't know Him at all, I hope that you've come closer to Him. Maybe you've met Him for the first time. Maybe you've just heard of Him for the first time, and He's caught your interest. That may not be you; maybe you have known Him for a while. If that's you, I hope that you've come closer to Him as well. Maybe there are things discussed in this book that you hadn't thought about before, and it's challenged your relationship with Christ. No matter how close or distant you feel you are to Christ, it's my hope that you've come closer to Him. I am thankful that you took the time to read what I felt like God wanted me to share. I hope the rest of your days are blessed with Him.

Author's Prayer

Dear God, I pray for the person reading this right now. I may not know them, but you certainly do. Please let them know how deep your love is for them. I pray that through this time they have spent reading, they have been brought closer to you. I pray that from this moment on, they will keep getting closer to you and that they will keep on growing in Christ. Let their relationship with you never stop growing as long as they're alive, just as the song "Oceans" says, let their faith go deeper than their feet could ever wander. Jesus Christ, there's nothing greater than you. Please help them see that great truth and truly want to live their lives for you. Give their hearts a desire and attraction toward you above all else. I pray this all in the name of Jesus Christ. Amen.

CPSIA information can be obtained
at www.ICGtesting.com
Printed in the USA
BVHW041538050820
585565BV00007B/507